Wallis: My War

WALLIS: MY WAR

– *A Novel* –

KATE AUSPITZ

QUARTET BOOKS

First published in the UK 2011 by
Quartet Books Limited
A member of the Namara Group
27 Goodge Street, London WIT 2LD

A catalogue record for this book
is available from the British Library

ISBN   978 0 7043 7228 3

Typeset by Antony Gray
Printed and bound in Great Britain by
T J International Ltd, Padstow, Cornwall

It is extremely difficult to write history . . .
it requires imagination.

ANATOLE FRANCE,
The Island of the Penguins

Contents

Introduction

Cleaners readying the Windsors' Paris *palais* for new tenants found this manuscript in a hat box. They gave the box and its contents to the agent who managed the property, and he brought them to me in great excitement. My husband and I had, from time to time, rented more modest lodgings from him, and we were living that year in one of his flats in the Marais close to the National Archives. He knew that I shared his interest in the 1930s and his admiration for the patriots who saw the Nazi threat clearly. He had been named for one of them, Georges Mandel, shot by a Vichy militia in 1944.

He did not doubt that the box and all it held – some papers, a notebook, and two bound books – came from the Windsors' house on the boulevard Suchet. The cleaning *équipe* had worked for him for years. It was possible that someone might have planted it and imposed upon them, but it was unthinkable that these honest Bretons would seek to deceive him. They did not ask for money. They brought their trove to him, I imagine, because they liked him and recognized him, as my husband and I did, as a serious person with an inquisitive turn of mind. He thought the whole thing might be a hoax, but he wanted me to see it. On the cover of the notebook, 'The War Memoir of HRH Wallis, Duchess of Windsor' was handwritten in large block letters.

I had never been much interested in the Duke and Duchess of Windsor, who struck me, quite apart from their supposed Nazi sympathies, snobbery, and idleness, as having led the most pointless lives imaginable. I knew next to nothing about them, apart from what I imagine most people know: that the Duchess schemed before her marriage and until her death to be addressed as 'Her Royal Highness' and that she had been buried at Windsor in a coffin that did not bear those coveted letters. The title *HRH Wallis, Duchess of Windsor* therefore piqued my interest.

Georges read English and he had tried to make out the rest, but the handwriting and the slang confounded him. He was not sure what to make of the other items in the box, and we went through them together. I recognised one of them at once: the Christmas photograph of Queen Elizabeth sent in 1939 to every man and woman in the armed forces. My husband's uncle, who fought in the Czech Brigade, kept his with his medals. This portrait had been childishly defaced. Someone had given the Queen horns, moustache, and goatee and blackened two of her front teeth. Another card, lurid red poinsettias blooming beneath a neon green palm tree, read 'Merry Christmas from Hollywood. Come up and see me some time, Mae West.' There was a picture postcard of Westminster Abbey, postmarked around the time of the coronation of George VI, addressed to 'Mrs Wallis Warfield Simpson,' the correct usage for divorcees in that period, at a château in France: 'Wish you were here! xxoo J.'

'Kisses and hugs,' I explained to Georges. 'Somewhat juvenile, but affectionate and perfectly *convenable.*'

More formal, in black ink on a folded sheet of thick white paper with a Tiffany watermark: 'Wallis, my dear, I am so sorry. I would not have thought such a thing possible. With deepest sympathy, Kitty.' Undated. No envelope. Lastly, there was a photograph of some handwritten lines of verse, unfamiliar to me. 'Provençal?' Georges asked. I thought not.

The books were puzzling. One was the Anglican *Book of Common Prayer.* The Duchess might have owned one, I suppose, but nothing I had ever heard about her hinted that she was even conventionally religious, certainly nothing to suggest that this book would be a cherished possession. So far as I knew, she had never made any pretence of piety even as a widow, when fashionable women often affect devotion. There were no marginalia, but some people are superstitious about writing in a Bible or a prayer book, and it struck me, uncharitably, that I was far readier to believe her superstitious than reverent.

The other book, the first volume of the pre-war *Guide Bleu* for Italy, *Des Alpes à Rome*, did reveal a trace of personality, but only just. On the flyleaf, a hand different from the one in the notebook had written 'p. 102'. Four characters only, not much to go on, but it seemed to be written by another person; none of the dates in the notebook resembled these numbers. My friend had noticed this annotation too and, triumphantly, he took the book from me and turned to the page. '*Voilà, madame!* Three stars. The destination is worth the trip.' In the margin, next to a description of a beach near Portofino where I had never been, three stars had been sketched.

I asked Georges to stay for supper, and after he left and my husband went to bed, I began to read the memoir. I read it through in one night. It was titillating and I am not above gossip, though I am, so to speak, methodologically opposed to celebrity history. Nonetheless, the story fascinated me, and the more I read, the more plausible it seemed.

The Duchess who had never interested me became enthralling. I was busy with a scholarly project, but she would not leave me alone. I bought and read her autobiography, *The Heart has its Reasons*, condescending to the woman all the while. Who had suggested that line from Pascal? How cynical could a publisher be?

It was painful to read: she had always behaved with perfect propriety, although she confessed to being gay and flirtatious. Her first two husbands were unsatisfactory, the first violent and the second prosaic, but nothing was ever her fault. She was, in the beginning, merely flattered by the attention of the Prince of Wales and taken with the glamour of his position, but in time she came to love him deeply, chastely, until their union was sanctified, and their marriage could not have been happier. She regretted they had no children, that she had not experienced the 'miracle of creation' through motherhood. Her conduct was so perfect that one almost suffocated reading about it.

Plainly, that book had been ghostwritten, and who knew if she'd even read it? Unsatisfied, I ordered the collection of letters written during their 'courtship'. The Prince of Wales revealed himself to be quite as bad as one imagines, cognitively and emotionally challenged, people would say today. Wallis Simpson, however, particularly in her letters to her aunt and confidante Bessie Merryman, was a revelation: shallow, selfish, grasping, a woman part Becky Sharp, part Lorelei Lee, and nobody's fool. She wrote to her aunt in the voice one hears in this memoir. Vulgar: 'the world is going to the bow-wows'. Narcissistic: she wanted to see everything written about her in the United States during the period the British press kept silent about her relationship with the heir to the throne. Contemptuous of 'the boy,' she seethed with rage that, Prince and King, he remained in thrall to his mother. Her resentment towards the woman who became the Queen Mum revealed more pure class hatred than most Marxists would impute to a seduced and abandoned factory girl.

But isn't genteel poverty always more galling than simple want? Wallis Warfield's father, with some pretensions to antebellum Southern aristocracy, died when she was an infant. Her mother, she said, married three times simply to keep a roof over her head. What was a girl like Wallis to do? A wealthy uncle paid her school fees, but such education as she got did not fit her to support herself. Should she have learned typing and shorthand? Become a saleslady in a smart shop? Not while her social connections sufficed to find eligible husbands. She played the cards she held and won the jackpot. It was hard not to feel a grudging admiration.

The Duchess appears, for most of her manuscript, oblivious to the historic events in which she participated. She repeatedly insisted that she knew and cared nothing about politics, and even after D-Day she wrote, 'I never claimed credit for the success of the Normandy landings, though they were a success. I was never ambitious in that way.' She wanted to be Queen of England, but resourceful and determined men bullied her into forcing the King's abdication. They knew that Edward VIII would not and could not fight the war that had to be won. They pressed her into service again and again, and she grew more conscious of her role; but only after the war, when her divorce lawyer reappeared as a judge at Nuremberg, did she glimpse the extraordinary brilliance and ruthlessness of the Anglo-American elite and of the French republicans with whom they were intimately linked.

The victors were, above all, thorough. They marshalled every resource, military, political, diplomatic, and literary and artistic culture, both high and low, to defeat the Axis: the interventionists worked in perfect sympathy and with consummate skill. Eton and Groton and the best of the French put their heads together and got it done. The isolationists and appeasers were outsmarted and outclassed. It was not the Cunning of History that made use of Wallis Simpson; it was the best brains of the civilized world, as she somewhat unwittingly relates.

In the end, I came to believe the manuscript was genuine. I had read the letters and memoirs of several of its principal figures, and the more I read of the other men and women she knew, the more convinced I became. I concluded that the notebook should be published and, insofar as possible, authenticated. When the Duchess's recollections are supported by other contemporary accounts, I have given the citation in a footnote. Much cannot be corroborated, and readers must judge for themselves how much is true and how much imaginary.

Her memoir, not surprisingly, reveals all the unthinking prejudice and casual racism of her period and her set, so shocking to rightminded people today. The Duchess used words like 'pansy' herself and unselfconsciously reported other persons saying 'Wog' and 'Dago', as no doubt they did. She never, in fact, used the 'N-word', preferring 'darkies', better suited to the Southern-lady persona she adopted to explain her family's reduced circumstances. Her freedom with ethnic epithets is counterbalanced, however, by her delicacy with regard to sex. Political correctness, for all its comic turns of phrase, has purified our discourse, and this text could benefit from it. On the other hand, the Duchess could write of love without pornography, and there is much to be said for that. And love she did, if this story is to be believed. Love brought her the agony of loss, suffered by many millions of others during those terrible years. No less than any other's, her exploits, her grief, and her revenge deserve to be remembered.

Wallis: My War

Chapter One

Harold Nicolson broached the idea of removing the King one evening in Biarritz. He was one of those people the Brits pay attention to. They may or may not be rich. They may or may not have important jobs. But they matter. Nicolson and his odd wife were both writers, and he was a Member of Parliament too at that time, I believe, but I'm pretty sure he wasn't in the Cabinet. He was important, though, I knew that much, so when he asked me to come for a stroll, I thought I'd better do it.

He suggested we walk to the lighthouse. I remember it was the day after Bastille Day and mobs of people were heading in that direction, so I chose the path on the other side of the Casino that leads to Saint Jean de Luz. 'Even in fine weather, dear lady,' he said, 'we cannot see England from these cliffs.'

'*Tant pis*,' I said. I was wearing an ivory bias-cut crepe de Chine evening dress with a midnight blue shawl. 'Who cares?' As I shrugged my shoulders, my shawl slipped to reveal my fine collarbones and my canary diamond necklace.

'You do not, as our French friends say, regret England?'

'Have we French friends?'

'Dear lady, you have friends everywhere.'

I smiled. I do have friends everywhere. My necklace came from an Indian friend. I took it from his wife's jewel case one afternoon when she went out shopping and we stayed in. He had some servants flogged so I could keep it. The Kashmiri shawl he bought to encourage local industry. 'You would not mind never again to see fritillaries in an English meadow?'

'I'm not interested in birds. Nor do I care if I ever again see the – what's it? The worm in the cabbage or the scowl on Queen Mary's face. Queens ought to be more pleasant. One makes an effort.'

'Perhaps they ought to do. But as you bring it up, my dear, you cannot, you know, be Queen of England yourself.'

'I don't care so much, though I want to be Empress of India. I like Indians.'

Harold's eyes had a faraway look. 'So do I, dear lady, so do I. Splendid fellows. Better than Arabs, whatever some may say. That is why the French cling to Pondicherry. The wind,' he said, 'is sharpening for a gale. Come, let us take shelter in this convenient grotto. It might hold a madonna, a vision as you appear tonight in your white frock and blue wrap.' He was always gallant.

'That's the sticking point, isn't it? King's bride has to be a virgin or a widow?'

'Alas, yes.'

I remembered a few things about the Episcopal Church from boarding school.[1]

'If a woman's husband dies, she's a widow, right, even if they divorced before his demise?'

'I'm not much of a churchman, but I gather that's the view taken by the C of E.'

'Well?'

'But, dear lady, there are two of them, or there will be after your second divorce.'

'Surely his chums are up to that. My God, he was in some hotshot Guards regiment, wasn't he?'

'But two husbands? I remind you of Lady Bracknell's observation.'

'I haven't had what I'm sure is the very great pleasure of meeting Lady Bracknell.' I supposed she was one of those hateful old dowagers who won't receive divorced women.

'Of course you have not. She died before you were born, but she is remembered for saying, apropos an orphan, that to lose one parent might be deemed a misfortune but to lose two seems careless.'

Rather heartless, I thought. But they are tough, the Brits.

'What I meant to suggest is that one man might meet with an accident, but two accidents would not go unnoticed.'

Chapter One

'Josephine was divorced.'

'Indeed she was. I didn't know you'd read History.'

'Oh, it's generally known. *On dit.* My manicurist told me. Josephine was divorced, and Boney told the Pope to bugger off and he crowned her himself.'

'His Majesty is not – '

'Not Napoleon. No, he's not.' I didn't want him to think I was an utter fool.

'His Majesty is a Christian gentleman and, constitutionally, the Defender of the Faith. He could not' – he stopped and then resumed, as if steeling himself to something pretty bad – 'not love you so, loved he not honour more.'

'And you want me to give him up? Fat chance.' I would not be gotten rid of so easily.

'You misunderstand me entirely. You must marry him as soon as ever you can and you must absolutely reject any sordid half measures.'

'What sordid half measures?'

'A morganatic marriage, for example, in which your children could not succeed their father.'

Fat chance, I thought again. I'm not the motherly sort, and the boy is not a stallion. 'I might agree to that if you sweetened the deal. I'd take Empress of India.'

'Impossible.'

'Why?'

'Queen and Empress – the titles cannot be separated.'

'Why not?'

'It does not matter in any case. We'll have to grant India independence after the war.'

I had heard a lot of silly talk about war and I did not believe a word of it. 'The world is going to the bow-wows, is it?[2] You expect me to believe that? And because of this war of yours, the King can't marry me?'

'No, dear lady, because of the war he *must* marry you.'

Chapter Two

Nicolson said he would bring Duff Cooper for luncheon the next day so the three of us could talk. Tête-à-tête. I was pigging it in a rented villa with very few servants and an indifferent cook, so an intimate party suited me. Duff was Secretary for War or something like that. He was in the Cabinet, and he was married to one of the few really beautiful Englishwomen of her day. A duke's daughter, one of the girls the King ought to have married years ago, but somehow it hadn't come off. I'd had dinner with them and the King once or twice during the past months. He seemed a charming man, though bookish.

I ordered a simple menu: a cold soup, langoustines, which are always so good at Biarritz, a green salad, and peaches. I'd let the boys choose the wine when they came; the villa's cellar was pretty good, but the English butler was not. That left the rest of my morning free to look at the new press clippings that had just arrived from the States. My aunt Bessie Merryman and my girlfriends sent them, at my request.[1] It's important to know what people are saying about you. Others, not friends, sent them too, almost every day, and I must say there was no difference at all in what came from supposedly loyal and hostile sources. At first I tried to sort them – the gold-digger ones; my legions of other lovers, male and female; our pre-sumed sexual oddities (also his and hers, the King's and mine); the sermons about King David in the Bible and his sinful lust for another man's wife. It was too bad that the King's parents, who gave him five or six first names, chose to call him David. There were many religious rants about the emancipation of women and the destruction of the family and political rants about the Flapper vote.

One, sent by a girl I'd been at school with, quoted a man I'd never heard of saying that he'd be 'honoured to be selected to be the first Irish-American to represent the United States at the Court of St. James,' as he put it, 'but he could not ask his wife to dine with a tart.'[2] Polly had begun to write nice long gossipy letters, and a lot of the clippings came from her. But they were all so nasty that I gave up trying to organise them and I just separated them by where they came from. I kept them in hat boxes, big ones for New York and Washington, smaller ones for Boston, the Middle West, and California.

Harold and Duff were to come at one, and at noon I began to change for lunch. I decided on pale blue linen, sleeveless, with my new chalcedony bracelets set with cabochon sapphires.[3] I suspected they might think it common to wear faceted stones at luncheon. Both of their wives were extremely proper about dress, if not much else.

They were prompt and we had drinks on the terrace. Gin for them, champagne for me. We talked of this and that during the meal. There is a taboo among such people about talking business at meals. When we returned to the terrace for coffee, Harold began: 'You are a most extraordinary woman.' And he did not begin well, for any number of people had repeated to me his opinion that I was a 'perfectly ordinary American' who presented 'no danger.' And that the lovely dinners I planned for the King and our friends were 'second-rate'.[4] But I listened. People should never know how much you know about them. 'And your husband is a patriot.'

Duff Cooper spoke, with all his warmth and charm. 'He left Harvard in 1917 to volunteer for the Coldstream Guards.[5] The Americans who fought before you declared war meant a great deal to us all.'

'One hears too,' Nicolson said, 'that he is uxorious.'

'He is not.' I was furious. 'And even if he were, I don't see what's so bad about lending money and taking interest. Plenty of rich Christians do it every day.'

They were taken aback. Neither spoke for a minute or two. My defence of Ernest shamed them into silence. I was so sick of the rumours that my husband was a Jew. I think that possibly one of his grandfathers may have been, and his father was certainly a horrid old lecher, mean about expenses and very stingy with Christmas presents.[6]

Nicolson broke the silence. 'We are, as Oscar Wilde observed, divided by the same language. I've spent time in your country, as you know, dear lady.' I didn't know, but I continued to listen. 'There are words in common usage among us that you do not use. Like "lift" for "elevator".'

'Exactly.' The colour was returning to Duff Cooper's face. 'Or "boot" for the place one puts luggage in a car. Or "bonnet", for that matter, for the part that lifts up in front.'

' "Petrol," ' Nicolson proposed.

' "Petrol" indeed, and "lorry". '

' "Braces",' rather than "suspenders". '

' "Biscuits".'

I thought they would spend the rest of the afternoon compiling a dictionary, so I cut them short. 'Or "loo" for "powder room". I don't see what any of this has to do with my husband's religion.' I was still angry.

' "Uxorious", as we use it here,' Nicolson said, 'means that a man is devoted to his wife. Like our friend Duff, for example.'

'Easy to be devoted to Diana, I should say, and you worship Vita, old man.'

'Absolutely.'

I was glad they cleared that up, and they went on to say that it had never struck them before how much the word sounded like *usurious*, 'practising usury.' Quite another thing. Not the same thing at all. And no people had a monopoly on that, as I'd so rightly said.

'I see.' I'd have to check to find out if they were telling the truth, but for now, I decided to let it pass.

'What I had meant to say was that both of you – you, my dear, and the excellent Mr Simpson – cannot be supposed to be in the least ordinary people,' Nicolson began again.

I saw what they were getting at. 'I am not a man, if that is what you are hinting at so delicately.'

'I have always known that, my dear. You could not have fooled me,' said the famous pansy.

'No man could see you as anything but a beautiful and desirable woman,' Duff Cooper hastened to add. I had yet to hear of a woman in polite society he hadn't found desirable. 'We have come, alas, not to speak of love, but of war. It is coming, and soon. We are not ready. France is not ready. Hitler took the Rhineland while they were distracted by a bitter election. Blum's a brave man.'[7] He paused to make sure I was following.

'The little Jew who's premier now? Isn't he a socialist?'

'Yes, but not a fool. He sees the danger, though most of his party don't. They object to all forms of militarism except the one that will kill them as soon as it can.'

'And as a Jew, albeit a freethinker,' Nicolson said, 'there are things he can and cannot say about Hitler.'

'The King says Hitler poses no danger to England.' I had heard him say it time and again. War talk irritated him more than almost anything else. Lukewarm shaving water too, but few things irked him more. 'No danger to England whatsoever.' He'd made a speech last summer to the British Legion where he said nothing was worth fighting for, or words to that effect, and people talked about it for weeks.[8]

'I know.' They said it almost in unison.

Nicolson continued, 'The King, for all his excellent qualities, cannot remain where he is. Too many Tories share his point of view, and the danger grows greater every minute. A new German ambassador is due next month – Ribbentrop, who tacks a "von" onto his name and charms *arrivistes* as vulgar as he is himself.[9] And Heaven knows whom Roosevelt will send after the election. He may send Kennedy. He certainly owes him something for getting Coughlin off the air.'

They were talking to each other now, ignoring me. 'One hears he was useful when Pacelli was in the States, convincing him Coughlin was doing the Church no good,[10] and all in all, Roosevelt may think he's less dangerous in London than at home. My God, it could be Kennedy.'

'From Boston,' I said.

'You know him?' They spoke as one once more.

'No, I don't, but a school friend of mine does. She says he's a pig and a huge hypocrite. She saw his mistress at his house in Palm Beach, while his wife and several of his countless children were there for Easter.' That was the name, Kennedy. I would remember it.

'The two of you discussed this last night,' Duff said. 'And I entirely concur. The best plan is for the King to marry you and abdicate, or rather, to abdicate in order to be free to marry you.'

'But why should he have to abdicate? This prejudice against *divorcées* is so old-fashioned. At one time a divorced woman could not be presented at Court, and they've gotten over that. You just have to be innocent, the injured party.' I knew all about that. It had taken boatloads of documents from America. 'I was presented at Court five years ago.' I'd worn a lovely white satin dress and train, borrowed, funnily enough, from Thelma Furness. She was another American girl the silly boy was crazy about until she jilted him for Aly Khan. I added a *faux* aquamarine and crystal necklace and hair ornament to the outfit. I looked very nice. As everyone said, the dress looked better on me than on Thelma, and no one suspected my jewels weren't real, but I swore I would never, ever, wear fakes again.[11] I had a gold charm bracelet back then, of course, but nothing gem-studded to hang on it. Now I had a nice assortment, including a jewelled frog that would never turn into a man no matter how many times you kissed it.

'There is an immense difference,' one of them said, 'between bowing to the King and Queen and being the Queen yourself.'

The other elaborated. 'People have divorced women to dinner, or many people do. They are not the pariahs they once were, but no

Chapter Two

divorced person, man or woman, may be married in the Church of England.'

'It's simply not on,' Duff Cooper said. 'The shot is not on the board.'

'He wants to marry me, but why should I marry him if I can't be Queen? What would I do?'

'I've no doubt you could fill your days with delight, and not just domestic felicities – with many worthy and dignified occupations that would keep you in the public eye and make you universally admired and loved.'

'The underprivileged,' Nicolson said. Somebody'd warned me he was pink if not actually Red.

'Art,' Duff Cooper suggested. 'Patronage, connoisseurship, collecting.'

'He likes to design jewellery. He buys gems and gives a lot of thought to how I should wear them. He practically lives at Cartier when he's in Paris.'

'And those are happy hours,' Nicolson said. 'My friend is right that His Majesty is an aesthete, far happier with creative persons than with politicians.'

'He will be a happy man with you as his muse.'

'He could do all that and still be King. He's determined to brazen it out, and I don't see why he shouldn't.'

'He cannot be King of an England at war.'

'He doesn't want to be,' I reminded them.

'Gentlemen in England now abed will stay abed if it's up to him.' Hard words from Duff Cooper.

'It cannot be up to him,' Harold Nicolson said. 'It will not be up to him.'

'I'll think it over. But I don't see what's in it for me.'

The butler appeared at the French windows that led from the dining room onto the terrace. 'A call from London, madam, for the Secretary of State for War. Most urgent, they said.'

Chapter Three

Duff Cooper ran to the phone as quickly as a polite man can leave a lady and returned a few minutes later.

'There has been an attempt on the life of the King.[1] A constable seized the man before he was able to fire, thank God, and no one was hurt, but you see, my dear, time is not on our side.' He bent over me sweetly. 'Shall I ring for some brandy?'

I did not feel faint. After all, nothing happened, and I never bother about things that don't happen.

'If we don't remove him, others will,' Nicolson said.

I thought he might be bluffing, but for the moment I took his word for it.

'Who was it?' I asked.

'The man in custody is an Irish national.'

'That's a nice touch,' Nicolson said. 'With de Valera braying for a new constitution.[2] Very nice.'

'So, I repeat, my dear' – Duff had a lovely voice, a seducer's voice – 'the King can abdicate or someone will kill him. It's really up to you.'

I would not be pushed around. 'He's already settled a considerable sum of money on me.'[3]

'If he were to be murdered after abandoning his intention to marry you, you might be implicated. You cannot profit from a crime, you know, and plotting to kill the Sovereign's high treason.' Nicolson was stern.

'The Tower? Off with her head?' The Brits are tough, and they cling to their old customs.

Nicolson nodded. 'I am afraid so.'

Duff waited for that to sink in before he spoke. 'But reflect for a moment on something far worse. If our dear friend, His Gracious

Majesty, does not marry you now, the world would judge him a cad. For love of you, and for that reason alone, he can leave the throne with honour.'

'So York will be King and Shirley Temple will be Princess of Wales?'[4]

'Princess Elizabeth will become the heiress presumptive. The Duchess might yet have a son.'

'How old is she?'

'Thirty-six. She was born in the first year of the new century.'

Younger than myself, and most awfully wholesome. 'She appears to be blooming.' The first time I met her, she made us go ice-skating on a pond in Windsor Great Park.[5] My feet were freezing and my ankles ached and she kept whizzing round and round, saying how much she'd loved skating as a girl in Scotland. She wanted us to try Scotch reels on the ice. She was like the good girls at boarding school, happy, enthusiastic girls from rich old families who would never need to do anything in their lives but who did everything they were supposed to anyway. Polly was like that and we hadn't really been close at school. She only became a reliable pen pal after I settled in London. She wrote me about Nicky Longworth's death in 1931[6] while I was getting ready to be presented at Court. She herself was married to a man from Yale, rich and handsome, who belonged to all the right clubs and rode and sailed and played polo and tennis.

Harold Nicolson said he must go, had to see a man about a book he was publishing, and Duff tarried with me. We spent the afternoon together, and I must say, I understood why his wife chose him over the Prince of Wales. Girls with rich and powerful fathers can please themselves. Girls like Polly or Duff's wife or President Theodore Roosevelt's daughter Alice, who was married to Nicky Longworth. Girls who have to struggle to live decently and dress well and be introduced to people who matter must make sacrifices and take risks. My poor mother had to marry three times just to avoid living with relatives. Duff was very sweet that afternoon, tender and persistent, so at last I turned over and, still rather limp, agreed. 'OK. I'm in. What's next?'

'You know Count Ciano?'

'That story isn't true either.[7] I had Italian friends in China, but not him. I'd like to meet him, though.' I'd seen him in newsreels and he appealed to me. He looked very masculine, like my Argentine friend Felipe,[8] and people said he liked women. He was married to the boss's daughter, Edda Mussolini, and I wondered if she knew how lucky she was that her father was a dictator.

'Italy should be with us against Germany.'[9] Duff would repeat this again and again in those years. 'They would never have gone into Abyssinia if we'd opposed it firmly, in plain language. We ought to have closed the Canal,' he said. 'Good God, it would have been so simple.'

'The King was exasperated,' I remembered. 'We had to cancel our Mediterranean cruise last summer, and you would have thought Mussolini was invading Africa just to spite him.'[10]

'But you are going this summer. Next month. Diana and I are going with you.'

'Yes, on some fabulous yacht. Will you introduce me to Count Ciano?'

'I am told he is eager to meet you, and if you like, you could go to Alexandria too. You'll like Egypt. It's full of romance. Cleopatra, Caesar, Mark Antony. A world lost for love.'

It sounded like fun, and Duff suggested that, before we sailed, I ought to meet the novelist Somerset Maugham. I knew his wife, Syrie Maugham, the interior decorator who'd done my flat at Bryanston Court after I married Ernest and settled in London. She worked with Elsie de Wolfe, Lady Mendl, the most fashionable decorator in London.[11] Being their client was the easiest way to get to know the smart set. You paid them to come to your house, so, unlike some society women, they never refused.

Maugham happened to be in Biarritz just now, Duff said, and they could come round for drinks the next day at seven, if that suited me, and then we'd go out for a spot of supper. I thought I'd wear a white piqué dinner dress. Cotton is smart in the summer, so long as you wear it with plenty of pearls.

They turned up next evening as I was going through a new bunch of clippings from Polly. They'd come in the post with a note from the headmistress of our old school apologising for not keeping in touch. She'd gotten my current address from Polly Parsons Whitman, she wrote, and she hoped I had not forgotten the dear old place because Oldfields needed a new gymnasium. Both envelopes, the big brown one and the little cream one with the school's seal, were on the table by my *chaise longue.*

We all had long drinks. It was a hot night, and I had a big pitcher of *citron pressé* and lots of champagne on ice, and gin, of course. Duff Cooper said that Maugham and I had the East in common and we chatted for a time about gin drinks on which the sun was always setting. I'd been in China with, and then without, my first husband, so I could talk about Hong Kong and Peking and Shanghai. Maugham had been everywhere and for a time he spoke in some detail and at great length about places he'd been and people he'd met, and did I know Singapore, and had I ever run into old so-and-so? He was obviously fishing, but I wasn't sure for what. The old King had had me investigated and my 'China dossier'[12] was supposed to be shocking.

The truth was simple. 'I spent most of my time with an American couple, Herman and Katherine Rogers. I knew Katherine in California. She was a widow then, Katherine Moore Bigelow. She remarried and I saw them in Peking and they took me in when I escaped from my fiend of a husband.'[13]

Duff Cooper turned the conversation to our cruise, and Maugham said it was settled that I would meet Count Ciano in Rhodes while we were cruising off the coast of Turkey. 'The King does not care for ruins and he does not care for Dagos,[14] so you should be able to go ashore without him.'

'Diana and I are leaving the boat at Athens,' Duff said. 'I'll go to Rhodes and sound him a bit before you arrive.'

'Is there anything special you want me to say to him?'

'How much you like him,' Maugham advised.

'He's an intelligent man,' Duff said. 'Make clear to him that the one certain thing is that you and the King will be married. He'll be *au fait* with the Church–State issues. You should be frank that you want to be Queen but there's strong opposition and you're not sure the King can overcome it. If he can, Italy will have a steadfast friend in the Palace. If he abdicates, there will be a new King, who'll not care tuppence for Italy and who will see the need to fight the Germans.'

'Either way, it would be madness for Italy to cast her lot with Hitler,' Maugham said. 'That's the message, and it has the great advantage of being true. You might mention that the Duchess of York is a Scotswoman whose eldest brother fell at Loos.'

'Fergus Bowes-Lyon. Good God, that's right. She should be made Colonel-in-Chief of the Black Watch.'[15] Wheels were turning in the active brain of the Secretary of State for War.

'Will she wear a kilt?' I asked.

'I shouldn't think so. Why do you ask?'

'I was afraid it might not be becoming.'

'Oh, she's not the sort to care about that,' Duff said, and Maugham shot him a warning look. 'That is to say, she lacks your incomparable *chic*.'

It seems that Cookie, like Polly, appealed to a good sort of man. It made me tired to think about how hard I had to work to land the King, and what little joy I had of it. 'What's the plan for Egypt?'

'Piece of cake. You've just come from Rhodes, where a highly placed Italian promised he'd soon be making love to you on a barge on the Nile, like Antony and Cleopatra. Wealthy Egyptians holiday in Rhodes and everyone will know that you've spent time with the Foreign Minister.'

'I thought I was going to be alone with Count Ciano.'

Chapter Three

'He is the Foreign Minister at the moment,' Maugham said. 'Not that he won't cut his losses when the time comes.'

'Why will the Egyptians care about what he might do with me on a barge?'

'Because Libya and Abyssinia are merely staging grounds for an attack on Egypt. They will understand, moreover, that whatever the Italians are planning, the Germans would never trust Latins with the Canal. They'd occupy Egypt themselves, and that would not be very pleasant for the Egyptians.'

'The Germans are bad colonialists,' Duff added, 'and the King is a generous friend.'

'He is indeed,' I said, fingering my new necklace.

'And you, of course, deeply as you have come to love and admire Egypt, will make sure England keeps its promises.'

'Won't they know about the divorce problem?'

'The men you will be meeting are thorough cosmopolitans and understand European customs very well. They believe any man in the world will lie to any woman.'

'And vice versa, of course, naturally,' Duff chimed in. He was extremely fair-minded about sex.

'I know when men are lying,' I said.

'I've no doubt you do, and that will be helpful. The Egyptians may guess the King can't make you his Queen. You must convince them he'll be guided by you, whether or not you are his consort.'

'And who are these wise men?'

'Egypt is not Italy,' Maugham continued. 'The barges, so to speak, do not run on time and power is more widely dispersed. But I don't think you need to fascinate more than – what would you say, Duff, five or six?'

'I used to follow Egyptian matters fairly closely.[16] I'd say, at a minimum, to make sure the deal gets done . . . ' He rattled off names I could not catch, Ali Rashid Osman and Osman Ahmed Ali Wattle, Sinbad the Sailor, for all I knew. The only bit that was not unfamiliar that I heard over and over was, 'He's married to old so-and-so's daughter, remember? Charming girl, she was at Cheltenham when he was at Harrow.' That's the same old story all over the world.

'Well, it all sounds fascinating,' I said. 'As you said, the King doesn't like ruins and he thinks Wogs are worse than Dagos. As long as I bring enough jigsaw puzzles to keep him occupied on deck, I should be free to make as many friends in Egypt as I need.'

It was a terribly hot night and I went upstairs to freshen up before we went to supper. My dressing room overlooked the terrace and I could hear them talking. I could also see from my window that Somerset Maugham was reading my mail.

'Her old school chum is Skip Whitman's wife,' he said.

'It's curious,' Duff replied. 'Your wife met her five years ago and recognised her abilities. I wonder when the Bonesmen began to move in.'

'You think the Americans are running her?'

'Rogers is Herman Livingston Rogers. His family lives near Roosevelt's in the Hudson Valley and they must know each other. He went to Yale and had something to do with American intelligence during the war.[17] Most of all, it's hard to imagine spontaneous friendship between any woman Whitman would marry and Wallis Simpson.'[18]

'Simpson's been seen a good deal with the American wife of a French officer posted to Washington in 1916, another school friend, I believe.' Maugham was right. Mary Kirk Raffray, one of my bridesmaids when I married Win Spencer, had invited herself to our place in London and simply thrown herself at Ernest. Her clothes were rather naked for English taste, but, until this minute, it had never dawned on me to see Paris in her *décolletage*.[19]

'Our French friends leave nothing to chance.'

'Belt and braces. The more the merrier. She'll do good work in the Mediterranean.'

I came onto the terrace as quietly as I could and caught Willie with the Oldfields envelope still in his hand. 'Your school. I think? I

Chapter Three

was just reading the motto on its crest. Tasso, is it not?' he asked. 'How it must have inspired you as a schoolgirl.'

'They tracked me down to ask for money. As if I'd give them any. If the FBI ever needs your address, they contact the fund-raisers at your private school.'

They laughed and laughed, and we went to supper, a quiet little out-of-the-way place on the harbour in Saint Jean de Luz where they baked pieces of fish on plates in an oven. Duff toasted me at the end of the meal in the formal way. 'Gentlemen,' he said, though he was speaking only to Willie, 'I give you the Queen *manquée*.'

Things moved quickly after that. On July 23, just one week after the failed assassination, dear Ernest did the right thing. He went to a provincial hotel with a woman and ordered breakfast from room service so that waiters and chambermaids could give evidence of his adultery. This is what nice men did when their wives wanted a divorce. He was a lamb really and did *everything* that I asked him to do. I don't know if it was Mary Raffray or not, but he had her sign the register as 'Buttercup Kennedy.'[20]

Chapter Four

It was a challenge packing for the cruise, because I was going to be doing so many different things in so many different places. For Rhodes, I chose the violet lamé dress with the emerald green sash that attracted so much attention at the Duke of Kent's wedding.[1] Willie said that Mussolini had tarted up some old Crusader castle and made it appallingly vulgar,[2] so I gathered that Rhodes was not the place for understatement. Apart from that, I had my maid pack Schiaparelli evening dresses and several of Mainbocher's bias-cut silk slips and also his marvellous new halter-neck dress done in white piqué, fresh and daring, that I thought would be perfect for Egypt. I took lots of summery daytime frocks, and almost all my jewellery, and as I was selecting hats and gloves,[3] I remembered Oldfields. If I was going to visit classic sites, I ought to have a Latin tag to drop here and there. I'm no intellectual, but tossing off a quotation at the right moment can make quite an impression. I wasn't certain exactly what it meant, '*Fortezza, Umilitade e Largo Core*',[4] something about courage and humility, but if Somerset Maugham liked it, others might like it too. I called him to make sure I was pronouncing it properly and tucked the envelope into my make-up case so I wouldn't forget.

We set sail from Yugoslavia after meeting Prince Paul and his wife Princess Olga, who wore white linen and a pained expression during the entire time we spent together. Once at sea, we were a jolly party: the Duff Coopers, some others from our set, equerries and privates secretaries, and my American friends Herman and Katherine Rogers, who were added at the last minute.[5]

The yacht was enormous and perfectly appointed, the *Nahlin*, one of the largest motor yachts ever built in Britain, someone said. Our stateroom had been the library and the King had the bookshelves removed to make it more spacious.[6] He was a little self-conscious about books. 'At Oxford they said I would never be bookish but that I would learn from life,'[7] he told me early in our acquaintance. I suppose they had to say something. A college can't tell the King that his heir has the IQ of a radish. They wouldn't need to, of course, because the boy's mother had already broken the news.

With or without a library, the ship was greatly admired by all the kings and dictators we visited. None could match the King of England as a big spender, but King Carol of Romania managed to buy it outright some years later and I hope he had some fun with it before he was deposed. The official meetings and entertainments became more and more boring, and the King got more and more impatient with the endless formal hospitality. It was impossible to relax in sight of land. Equerries kept rushing up to tell him that he ought not to be seen in shorts, sandals, and undershirt – *singlets*, Diana Cooper called them. The King wasn't an imposing sight in *déshabille*, and his picture, looking like a scrawny slum urchin at a charity treat, would do the monarchy no good, or so they said. He dressed shabbily most of the time and he liked to go out in a dinghy with shrimping nets he found on some beach, 'like a child of eight,'[8] Diana said, and catch jellyfish. I did not take an interest in this, but most of the others encouraged him. They would lean over the rail and shout, 'There's a big one, sir. Over there, can't you see it?'

Duff and Diana left the boat as planned at Athens, and that was a relief. I never saw such people for monasteries and goat paths to nowhere. One day the King and I went with them and we walked for an hour up stairs cut into a cliff to see 'a view' and some statues.[9]

I was ready for a change and looked forward to Istanbul. Harold Nicolson predicted I would find Atatürk attractive. He was in favour of women being undressed or something like that, and everybody thought it very modern and progressive, and I imagine he made good use of the policy himself. Personally, I did not fancy him. I liked the look of Turks in general, though, well-built and manly.

of a naked lady

We left Istanbul and sailed round the coast of Turkey, and one afternoon when the King was engrossed in a particularly tricky jigsaw puzzle,[10] we caught sight of Rhodes. The island of roses, as someone called it. A bunch of us were keen to see it, but the King wanted to finish the puzzle and Herman and Katherine Rogers volunteered to keep him company. I was given leave because I'd never been to Rhodes before. The landing party met on deck after luncheon. I'd decided to wear yachting clothes, beige linen slacks and a white silk shirt, and to have my maid come along with a change of clothes in case Duff had arranged the meeting with Count Ciano for that night. I brought a gorgeous necklace to wear with the Kent wedding dress, a cascade of big amethysts and turquoises, with coloured diamonds and rubies and a black opal or two.[11] Maugham emphasised that no expense had been spared in the restoration of Rhodes, and it's important, when travelling, to be in harmony with the various décors.

Our group toured the old and the new cities, the marketplace, the aquarium, the Yacht Club. The afternoon wore on and when the others were thinking about getting back to the boat for 'KTs', the cocktail hour they looked forward to more than dinner, Duff Cooper materialised. A special *cicerone* had been found, he said, to show Mrs Simpson the Palace of the Knights. He hinted, without actually saying so, that it was the King's wish that I tour the palace privately, because palaces were made for me and me for palaces, so to speak, and it was all very hush-hush so they shouldn't speak of it. He was good at his job, Duff Cooper.

He found a place for me to change and, as the sun was setting, escorted me to the Palace of the Knights of Saint John. A man in a dinner jacket was waiting beneath a high arched entry-way and he stepped forward to meet us. 'Mrs Simpson, Count Galeazzo Ciano di Cortellazzo,' Duff Cooper said, bowed, and retired.

The Count drew my hand through his arm, and we walked through the arch into an enormous courtyard and then into the palace itself, through long corridors, more arches, coats of armour, swords, axes, spears, shields, everything very big and brightly coloured. 'We think it was all polychrome originally,' the Count said, in very good English. 'The Middle Ages were bloody, after all. So we did not aim for *grisaille*.'

'It's all very nice and bright,' I said. 'And clean. A lot of the Mediterranean is too dirty for my taste.'

He smiled as if I'd made a joke. 'It is clean, with all modern conveniences. Il Duce installed central heating, as you see.' There were steam radiators everywhere, at the end of marble corridors, set into mosaics, jutting out beneath tapestries. They seemed to embarrass the Count, who was more attractive in person than in pictures.

'They must make it cosy in the winter.'

'To find such irony with such beauty,' he said, looking at me the way I like men to look at me. 'You are a Futurist, perhaps? You prefer modern things?'

I had no idea what a Futurist was, so I stuck to something I knew. 'I like aeroplanes, but they frighten me terribly.'

Duff told me the Count volunteered to serve as a pilot in the Abyssinian war.[12] My first husband was an aviator too. He was a brute and he drank and I couldn't live with him, but I'd liked him a lot when we first met. Count Ciano reminded me of him a little, and I wasn't surprised when he asked, 'Does it please you to be frightened, Mrs Simpson?'

'Sometimes.'

I took to him immediately and he seemed taken with me. I was glad I had changed for the evening, because he flattered me, as I'd hoped he would. I looked like a Queen, like Cleopatra. He actually said that: 'Cleopatra, clad in barbaric splendour.' Seeing me, a man wanted to kill leopards and drape their skins over my shoulders. His voice became almost a growl as he spoke of this, and seemed to promise that he would take the clothes off too, before very long.

'I'd like a leopard skin very much.' Of course, I didn't tell him I already had a lovely leopard sport coat.[13] The King hadn't killed the animals, needless to say. I bought the skins with the first money he gave me to spend on myself and had the coat made in London. 'Your palace is splendid, and not at all barbaric.'

'Not with the renovations,' he said. 'It has enough plumbing for a block of flats.' He smiled rather sadly. 'Tell me, Mrs Simpson, what do you, so beautiful and sophisticated, really think of all this? Tell me, honestly, what is in your heart, being here in this place?'

'Being here with you, Count? It makes me believe in "*Fortezza, Umilitade e Largo Core*".'

He was stunned. 'To hear Dante's words on such lips. I have never met anyone like you.' Oldfields had finally done me some practical good. I decided to send them five dollars for their new gym. 'If you know that poem, you must know Ovid too,' he said. 'Tell me, which do you prefer, *The Metamorphoses* or *The Art of Love*?'[14]

'Can't you guess?'

The rest of the evening was wonderful. I'd had lots of beaux and I'd never, ever felt the way I felt that night. It may sound silly, but it's true. It was hard to leave him, but I couldn't stay on Rhodes overnight. The King would be anxious if I did not return, so we made a rendezvous for the next day.

The Count came for me in a small sailboat while the others were at lunch. He looked like a fisherman and I was bare-legged, wearing a pale green dress, a fine lawn, embroidered with daisies, and a wide-brimmed white straw hat. I'd told the King I'd found a cunning little shop while sightseeing the day before. Sandals, pottery, local handicrafts. The owner's son was going to pick me up and bring me back and I would not dream of troubling the crew to take out the tender. The King was keen to finish the puzzle now that he'd located the odd-shaped piece he'd been hunting for all morning. He was happy, a pin-up girl was taking shape as he worked, and he told me to have fun and not tire myself.

I went over the side on a rope ladder. The ship's accommodation ladder was meant to rest on a substantial boat, not a tiny skiff. At least fifty of the crew watched me, all grinning broadly. The King thought they were touched by my consideration, unwilling to take them away from their duties for my afternoon of shopping. Willie Maugham told me later it was something called *ressentiment*. The crew would be royalist to a man, he thought, but pleased to see a poor man make a fool of a toff.

We sailed to a little cove where there were lots of wild rose bushes. The Count said it was true, there were always roses on Rhodes, and pointed out a grove of trees beyond, which he said I would like. It was very private. I asked him, as we walked among the flowers, if he had a nickname. Galeazzo was rather a mouthful. He said some people called him Gallo, and gave me a pleased sort of look. 'You agree?'

I hadn't the faintest idea what he meant. Willie told me later that *gallo* meant 'cock'. 'It's very nice,' I said. 'Very musical. Italian words always sound so pleasant.'

He laughed. 'I should not, what do you say, fish for compliments. But perhaps I will be able to convince you.'

My mind wanders at certain times, and I was wondering later that afternoon what Mussolini's daughter was like. People said she was a chip off the old block, with a vile temper. I could write a book, I was thinking: *Son-in-Laws I have Known*. Taken as I was with what was happening, I blurted out, 'How do you say "son-in-law" in Italian?' He shut my mouth with a kiss. 'No, really, tell me.' If I have a fault, it is that, tactful as I can be when I must be with people I don't care about, I am as thoughtless as a child with people I like.

'Not now.'

'I want to know.'

He got a little rough then but quite marvellous, and afterwards he said, '*Genero*. And "father-in-law" is *suocero*. Mine is a Great Man, as he says himself.'[15]

'Come to me tonight,' he said as we sailed back to the yacht. 'There is a performance of *Aida* in the courtyard of the palace. Bring a party from the boat, and you can slip away after the first act.'

'Do you know how it ends?' He thought I was the wittiest woman in the world, but I wasn't joking. 'The King might ask.'

'Doesn't he trust you?'

'Of course he trusts me. He likes me to tell him stories.' Sometimes I didn't know if he needed a wife or a nanny.

'Scheherazade,' he said. 'Happy man. How good it must be to be the King of England.'

The opera was about Egypt and Abyssinia, oddly enough, and I suppose Mussolini commissioned it to celebrate his victory.

'What's it like there?' I asked. We were refreshing ourselves with wine and fruit after some hours together and people were still singing at the top of their lungs in the courtyard. Operas take a long time and I had never been so pleased that they did. 'You were in Africa, weren't you? How was it?'

'It was good, except for the Germans. I had some in my squadron. To learn about our planes so they could tell us how to fly them.'

I thought that was enough conversation and tried to recapture his attention, but he could not stop talking about the Germans, the contempt they'd shown for his officers, their gross discourtesy to the lower ranks, their disdain for any piece of machinery made outside the Fatherland, the things they insisted on eating and drinking regardless of the climate, their inability, which caused endless trouble, to tell the difference between native girls from respectable families and the other sort. 'The worst ones,' he said, 'pretended to like Italy and constantly quoted Dante.'[16]

I said I was guilty of that myself, and he smiled. 'That was different. You are different.' I hoped after that he'd make love to me again, but he wasn't finished with the Germans. 'One evening,' he said, 'we took off at sundown to practise night flying by instruments, and one of them saw a leopard, moving out from some rocks. Moving so beautifully. Magnificent. There is nothing so elegant as a leopard.'

Chapter Four

'I like leopards too, and panthers.'

'He strafed it. It exploded in blood. You cannot imagine.'

I was shocked. The hide must have been worthless. I didn't know what to say. Most English people would have had a lot to say.

'I chased him out to sea,' he said. 'And shot him down.'

There was a dinner at the yacht club our last night off Rhodes. The King's staff insisted he attend because it would mean a great deal to the locals. Duff Cooper said I must be there too. There had to be some public introduction, so I could remain in contact with Count Ciano if the need arose. I wore one of my bias-cut crepe de Chine dresses, a deep blue. With it I wore the flower head necklace[17] that went with the chalcedony and sapphire bracelets. Against the dark silk, the tiny diamonds set into the sapphires really dazzled, and I wore the ear clips too. It was one of my most effective summer outfits. The party, sad to say, was very tense and dull.

The Count greeted us on behalf of Il Duce and of Victor Emmanuel, King of Italy and Emperor of Abyssinia, whose regret that he was unable personally to welcome his brother King and Emperor was incapable of expression. The King said he regretted it too, and gave Gallo a look that left no doubt how sorry he was to be dining with him at all.

I had the place of honour at the right of the host, but because we were supposed to have just met, we had to be very formal. Gallo's manners were perfect. He could have been an Englishman. He did not so much as touch my hand.

His Countess wasn't there, so the plump wife of some local notable graced the other end of the table and tried to make conversation in French with the King, who was fidgeting and, from time to time, managing '*Sans doute*' or '*Exactement*'. He had trouble understanding aldermen's wives in England too, as he'd often said, but this dinner was more than usually wearing.

'I didn't like the looks of that son-in-law,' he said as we were getting ready for bed. 'He behaved very respectfully to you, I was glad to see, but you know his reputation.' I knew what people said about Count Ciano. I'd heard all about his conquests, and I was happy to be one of them.

'I'm ready for drowsels [18] now,' the King told me after he had brushed his teeth, so I tucked him in and read him *Winnie the Pooh* until he fell asleep. That was a book he liked. Sometimes he read by himself books about Bulldog Drummond where all the villains were swarthy.

The *Nahlin* had engine trouble as we attempted to sail away and I announced that I had a toothache and must see an English dentist. The closest one was in Alexandria. The equerries and private secretaries absolutely forbade the King an unannounced or incognito visit to Egypt. I told him I was in terrible pain and a Royal Navy destroyer, the HMS *Bacchante*, was sent to ferry me back and forth. I expected to return to the yacht when it was ready to sail.

Alexandria was livelier than Rhodes. Willie Maugham met me there. He knew all the hotels and restaurants and bars, and everyone in them, including the waiters and bartenders. We spent a lot of time on the Corniche, a pretty beach that goes for miles along the harbour. I wore linen and cotton in Egypt, rarely silk. It was very hot during the day. Everyone looked forward to the cooler evenings, and the city was as gay as Budapest or Prague. Every evening we met a group of friends for dinner, sometimes at a new and modern hotel, the Cecil, in the centre of town and sometimes at the old Metropole by the sea.

I didn't care very much about anybody I met, although the men could not have been more charming. Achmed, the nicest, was the son-in-law of the Minister of the Interior, a position Willie said was like being the Chief of Police for all of Egypt and the Lord High Executioner all in one. He was the best-looking, in a blue blazer and an Old Harrovian tie. He was not the best lover but by far the most

Chapter Four

amusing company, and he is the only one of the Egyptians I remember distinctly.

There were so many of them, and they were so alike. Besides Achmed, there were Ibrahim, Rashid, Wazim, Suleiman, quite a lot of dusky charmers, and one gorgeous blue-black Nubian who'd studied chemistry in Aberdeen. He asked me if it was true that the King liked to play the bagpipes at night. I was surprised he knew about that and said it was true, he not only played the pipes, he composed for them.[19] 'An ancient art, Mrs Simpson,' he said, smiling with a flash of very white teeth. 'We will show you some other ancient arts.'

They all wanted me to come back in the fall when migrating quail fell onto the beach. They caught the birds in nets, they said, and plucked and gutted them right there and grilled them over bonfires lit on the sand. The sea reflected the fires on the beach and the air smelled of roast bird and burnt spices, and everyone had a good time all night long in all the places where the fires did not shine. Some British people thought it unsporting, but they were sure I would enjoy it. Willie agreed it was great fun and he hoped, before too long, the King and Queen of England would join them for it.

He was with me most of the time, talking of the Suez Canal and the headwaters of the Nile and the dangers Egypt faced from Italy and Germany. I confirmed the presence of Germans in Abyssinia, and Achmed listened carefully. 'An authoritative source told you this, Mrs Simpson? Recently?'

'Authoritative but impertinent,' Maugham said, with a look like an old maid. 'A highly placed Italian had the effrontery to say to this lady . . . ' Gallo's supposed boast that he would make love to me on a barge in the Nile always made a big impression, and I tried to blush when Willie spoke of it. But it's never been easy for me to blush. I'm pale, and even as a debutante I had to rely on rouge.[20] The Egyptians promised gory vengeance on any man who dared insult me. The Nubian swore he could cut such a villain where it most mattered, cover him with wild honey, and sink him in a pit full of red ants. Achmed said, 'I give you best,' and the others cheered, 'Well done, the Upper Nile!' The hoorays were so rousing that other guests at the Metropole complained about the disturbance.

Aida made a hit every time. They seemed to think it was all very sinister and they asked again and again about details of the performance. Willie, who really ought to have produced shows, kept coming up with funnier and funnier ideas about the staging. The opera had been performed in modern dress, he said, the chorus in black shirts, riding in tanks, not on elephants, the High Priest dressed as the Pope. I didn't get all his jibes, but the Egyptians hung on his words and howled with fury. Veins throbbed on their foreheads and they clenched their fists and pounded them on the tables. 'And yet,' Achmed said one evening, 'it was clever of the Italians, an apt tribute to you, Mrs Simpson. *Nel mio pensiero tu sei regina.* In Egypt too, in our thoughts and in our hearts, you reign as Queen.'

I told the leopard story often, leaving out the Count, and it always stunned them. Willie generally added that the Germans strafed villages too, but the leopard seemed to interest them more.

'Such gratuitous cruelty,' one of them said. I think he'd been at Oxford or Cambridge.

'Not sporting,' another agreed. 'It cannot be compared with netting birds.'

'I myself have killed a leopard with a spear,' my chivalrous Nubian said, and he certainly looked as if it might be true.

'It's just stupid to destroy the pelt.' They were a practical lot, by and large. Like Americans, but with less get-up-and-go.

'Their guns must be good,' Achmed said. 'A leopard would present a difficult target from the air.'

I liked them, but I was losing interest in Egypt. I was trying to figure out how I could manage a weekend at Lake Como before I had to get back to England. Willie always knew when my mind was

Chapter Four

wandering and he'd draw me back into the conversation. He kept urging me to tell my new friends how greatly the King respected their prowess. I felt they should not be encouraged to believe the King had inclinations in that direction.

All in all, my visit turned out to be a success. A few days after I got back to the yacht, word came from London about an Anglo-Egyptian Naval Treaty.[21] The King and I were having a late breakfast on deck when an equerry brought the wire. 'Just as well to have them on our side, I suppose. But we shan't need them for anything,' he said, handing the paper back.

A little package was waiting for me when we put into port at Dubrovnik, a charm for my bracelet, a dear little golden sphinx with emerald eyes and *W R I* inscribed between its feet.[22] Nothing more, just the letters. I thought it odd that only three of my Egyptian friends, Wazim, Rashid, and Ibrahim, had signed it. Possibly the really influential and well-connected ones, like Achmed, were afraid to compromise themselves, even with an initial on a bauble.

I showed it to Willie when I got back to London, and he laughed. 'WRI – Wallis *Regina et Imperatrix*, Queen and Empress. They may know it isn't in the cards, but no matter.'

Chapter Five

I am a flirt[1] and always have been. When Win Spencer was an aviator during the Great War, people said I'd never met a pilot I didn't like. I was the life of the party in Pensacola and San Diego and everywhere else we went, and the best proof of it was the chilly treatment I got from the other officers' wives. I was curious, naturally, about Charles Lindbergh and keen to meet him when Colonel and Mrs Lindbergh invited us to a dinner party they were giving for the new German ambassador. Joachim von Ribbentrop, after years of angling for the job, finally got it around the time we returned from our cruise.

There were even then a lot of stories about Ribbentrop and myself, which he did his best to promote, and the Lindberghs invited us at his request. The newspapers that still approved of the King said his willingness to be a guest in private homes showed what a modern monarch and true democrat he really was.

I wore a new dress, a marvellous black satin *charmeuse* creation from Coco Chanel. Her street clothes were divine and I take credit for encouraging her to design evening gowns as well. The dress was the perfect foil for my gorgeous Prince of Wales diamond brooch, the three white plumes of the crest done in diamonds and set above a gold coronet.[2] The boy was King now, and no longer Prince of Wales, but I liked to be seen as sentimental about such things. My aunt Bessie, always a source of excellent advice, sent me butter moulds with this emblem[3] shortly after we became friends. I used them every time I entertained and they were much noticed and helped establish me in London society.

Nicolson was there when we arrived and said I was looking well after my time at sea. 'Smashing diamonds,' he said, 'though one white feather would do for tonight.' Mrs Lindbergh was busy with arriving guests. Bad weather had delayed her husband's flight from Berlin and he was said to be dressing for dinner.

That evening's hottest topic was Jessica Mitford, one of the wild daughters of Lord Redesdale. She'd run off with a Communist to fight in Spain, and at that point nobody knew if she'd bothered to marry him first. Those girls were quite a bunch. One was supposed to be in love with Hitler and another left her husband for Oswald Mosley, head of the British Union of Fascists, and married him, as soon as she could and not a minute too soon, at the home of the Minister of Propaganda in Berlin.[4] 'Not what one expects to hear, eh, from daughters of an English peer,' Harold Nicolson said. 'Redesdale is hedging his bets.' He got me another glass of champagne and manoeuvred me into the library. I'd heard that Mrs Lindbergh liked to read.

'Why are you here?' I asked him. 'Are you and our hostess soulmates?'

'I wrote a biography of her late father. He was American ambassador to Mexico, self-made millionaire, interesting chap, and the Lindberghs will be renting our house in Kent.[5] What's the story about you and Ribbentrop?'

'I met him last year at Emerald Cunard's during the Silver Jubilee,[6] she's expected here tonight, and he's been sending me flowers ever since.'

'Seventeen flowers?'

'Yes. Seventeen every time, no more, no less. The American papers are full of it.' Polly Whitman had asked me about it several times, and so had Katherine Rogers. 'They don't know if he sends roses or carnations, but they know it's always seventeen.'

'What does it signify?'

'I haven't the faintest idea.'

'Did you meet him on the seventeenth of some month?'

'No, nor in his or in my seventeenth year. The American papers say it's the number of times we've made love. But you'd think, wouldn't you, that the number would increase or the man would eventually stop sending flowers?'

'Dashed odd. He's a scheming little wretch, though, must be something. He's been asked about it many times and he looks sly and says he cannot comment.'[7]

'He's a worm, and you know what I think? He does it to make people think there is something between us, and refusing to talk about it makes him look like a gentleman.'

'Very possibly. He's doubtless lied to his own people about his relations with you in order to be sent to London. We'll spoil his fun,' Nicolson said. 'There's a man I'd like you to fascinate tonight to get his goat.'

'Colonel Lindbergh himself?'

'No, I fear he will be deaf and blind to your charms and you won't like him much either. But you'll like Freddy. He's an attaché who'll arrive with Ribbentrop, Graf Friedrich von und zu . . . ' His name was impossible to pronounce or remember, and I'm not sure what became of him. If he's still alive, I wouldn't want to embarrass him. He was a very nice boy.

'He is everything his chief is not,' Nicolson said, 'and it will drive Ribbentrop wild to see you flirt with him.'

It did indeed. Freddy, who did not like his English friends to call him Fritz, was well above six feet tall, blond, blue-eyed, pink-cheeked but not the least cherubic, his brow and jaw were fine and virile, and his young body was all arms and legs. He held himself well, but when he clicked his heels it was like watching a marionette. Someone pulled the strings and his heels clicked. It didn't look like something he'd bother to do himself. When we were introduced, he told me how much he liked the United States. Lindbergh did not appear and the KT hour went on and on, so we had time to get acquainted.

'I've just come from Washington.'

'You had a good time there?'

'Terrific. I stayed with my American cousins. All the educated

Chapter Five

members of my family were expelled from Prussia in the last century. If I came from highbrows instead of simple soldiers, I might be in Congress now myself. Though,' he continued, meeting my eyes with his frank and cheerful gaze, 'I'm too young yet to be the Speaker of the House.'

That surprised me. We'd been very discreet. I was young then myself and not yet divorced, and Nicky Longworth was, as Freddy said, the Speaker of the House. His wife, Alice, was involved with a senator named Borah and people called her Aurora Borah Alice. I think senators are more important than Nicky was, but he was always treated like a VIP, so I assumed he must be rather important too in some way.

'You know all about our politics?'

'I'm supposed to, and your history and customs too. Washington's a Southern city, isn't it, gracious and easy-going, not a Puritan town like, say, Boston.'

'Boston's not so puritanical these days.'

'So one hears, and you yourself are a Southern lady, are you not?'

I was born in Pennsylvania and I grew up in Baltimore, but Elsie Mendl had advised me to be as Southern as possible in England. It would set me apart from the rich Yankee girls who were not much liked in the better circles. Besides, the great advantage of being Southern, as I'd known all my life, was that you could pass yourself off as coming from a good family no matter how poor you were. Your poor darling grandpa had been ruined by the carpetbaggers the way every Russian waiter and mannequin in Paris had been ruined by the Bolsheviks.

Freddy sympathised. Lots of families he knew had lost their estates. Times had been tough after the war.

Ribbentrop interrupted our chat, not at all pleased to find us together. 'It has been far too long,' he said, kissing my hand. 'How we all missed you, how I in particular pined for you when you were away. And how ravishing you look tonight, wearing the plumes of the Prince of Wales. All your admirers long to see you as Queen and as Empress. At last the Koh-i-Noor diamond will rest upon a brow more radiant than the jewel itself, and all your subjects, even the most benighted, will have, at last, a Goddess to worship.' He didn't know when to stop, and showed no sign of ever stopping when the King joined us. 'Your Majesty.' Ribbentrop bowed. 'Good evening. I was just saying how your Indian subjects will adore their Empress. You are planning a durbar after your Coronation to introduce your bride to the East? No doubt some of your Indian subjects worship her already.' I began to wonder just how good German intelligence might be. The Maharajah was not as careful as Nicky Longworth. He was an absolute ruler with no worries about the press, but our privacy was always guarded by a band of sturdy cutthroats who seemed devoted to him and terrified of the consequences of letting him down.

Dinner was, thank Heaven, finally announced.

The King sat at the right of Mrs Lindbergh, a sad, dowdy little thing, and I got the Colonel. Not much for small talk – he didn't seem to know I was there. He kept shouting down the table to the King about how well things were done in Germany. America, on the other hand, was a mess. Sensational newspapers got in the way of the police and they were as responsible as the kidnapper for his baby's death. Anne looked even sadder when he spoke about the baby and the need to muzzle the press. Ribbentrop knew that it was not the done thing to carry on in this way at a dinner party, and it was amusing to watch him, torn between his reputation as a gentleman and his responsibilities as the travelling salesman of the Fatherland. In the end, duty trumped vanity and he chimed in, giving examples and elaborating on all of Lindbergh's points.

The King had lately gone to Wales without me and he discovered while he was there that a lot of miners were unemployed. He'd told a reporter that 'something should be done.'[8] His observation was widely quoted and people who liked him said it showed he had a kind heart. There is some poem a lot of people know that says having a kind heart is better than having a crowned head. Ribbentrop praised the King's love for his people and his concern, expressed with such clarity and conviction, that 'something should be done.'

'Something certainly must be done,' Lindbergh said. 'Before the Bolsheviks take over another country, as Roosevelt and the Jews have taken over mine.'

'Men like you, Colonel, will take it back,' Ribbentrop said, and Mrs Lindbergh looked upset.

She flushed and spoke in a soft voice, her words coming quickly. The Depression was terrible, she agreed, but she was very much afraid that people suffered even more when constitutional government broke down. There was going to be an election in the fall and one could trust the people. She was most awfully earnest and went on and on. 'The United States has elections every two years for the House of Representatives and every four years for President. So we have every opportunity for gradual and non-violent change.' Senators served six-year terms, she concluded, and this gave the Upper Chamber *gravitas*, like the House of Lords.

I must say, she explained it all very clearly. I'd never grasped the details myself.[9] Her husband, however, seemed not to enjoy her lecture. 'There is a time, Anne,' he said, 'for action.'

'Of course, dear,' she said. 'You know best.' This time it was Nicolson who looked upset. The Lindberghs were a strange pair and I decided that Lindbergh was one pilot and one son-in-law I could skip.

'That is just the point,' Ribbentrop said. 'There is a need for action, "something should be done", as His Majesty has said, out of his deep love for his people and his matchless political acumen, and we cannot leave it to the Reds to do it. That is the beauty of National Socialism. It is national. It is what you call "blood and bones" and what we call "*Blut und Boden*". There is no rootless cosmopolitanism . . .'

'And very little socialism,' Freddy said, winking at me.

'As for our charming hostess's talk of elections . . . ' Ribbentrop did not respond to Freddy's joke, though I was sure he must have heard it. 'We all know that ladies may learn their lessons well and repeat them in later life like the good and pretty schoolgirls they once were, but ladies do not understand politics.'

'Many ladies understand politics very well,' Freddy replied, 'but they may not all care to discuss it at dinner. His Majesty is far too courteous to admonish his host, so it falls to me, as the only other representative of the old order, to insist on etiquette.'

His family must have been awfully important, because Ribbentrop simply glowered at him and said nothing. The King said he was quite right but the sufferings of his people affected him so deeply that he sometimes forgot himself. How he came up with that on the spur of the moment I will never know, and people nodded sympathetically.

Lindbergh said that decadent countries paid too much attention to etiquette and we all could learn from the *new* Germany. He stressed the 'new' as an insult to the young *graf*, I suppose, but Freddy smiled brightly. 'Right-oh, Colonel, and no man knows the new Germany better than you do.'

Emerald Cunard was a cut-up and a live wire and she could not resist teasing Ribbentrop. 'If politics is too dangerous,' she said, 'we can always talk about religion. Tell me, dear Mr Ambassador, what does Herr Hitler truly think about God?'

Ribbentrop replied that this was a deep subject that the Führer had under consideration and that he had not yet decided what doctrine would be best for his people.[10]

At this point, a British hostess would have simply gathered up the ladies and left the table. That poor child Anne Lindbergh tried to introduce another topic of conversation. British gardens were so wonderful, she said, bringing the subject up out of thin air. 'Charles and I so look forward to living at Seven Oaks. I hope to learn a great deal about gardening from Mr Nicolson and dear Miss Sackville-West, who couldn't come tonight. Their herbaceous

Chapter Five

borders are so wonderful. They really are an inspiration to us.' I wasn't sure if she meant the garden or the marriage, so different from her own.

Ribbentrop beamed. 'Gardens are the proper place for ladies. We know' – he leered at me –'how much the fair sex loves flowers and how happy they are to accept them as a pledge of our passionate devotion to them.'

Next morning, seventeen flowers were delivered – red roses this time. It was always red roses or white carnations. The man had absolutely no imagination. At about the same time, Freddy showed up with a bunch of daisies and invited himself to lunch. He told me that the embassy staff loathed Ribbentrop and called him Herr von und zu Keller, 'of and from the cellar,' because his money came from his wife, Annelies Henkell, the heiress to a champagne fortune.[11]

The King joined us for luncheon, and he and Freddy talked of Battenberg and Mountbatten cousins, and skiing and yachting and stalking and steeplechasing, with not one word about the suffering masses.

In the next weeks, I spent a lot of time in public with Freddy. We went all over London and its outskirts to places I'd never seen where there were always plenty of English day trippers and foreign tourists. We went to cathedrals. We went to Kew Gardens and to look at the Crown Jewels in the Tower. We went to Hampton Court, which had some connection with Henry VIII, a divorced monarch. Duff Cooper called after that outing to congratulate me. We went, one day towards the end of September, to the National Gallery to look at pictures. Freddy stopped in front of one of them and went on and on about the blues and the greens you saw only in Italian seas, and wasn't it curious that the chariot of Bacchus was being drawn by cheetahs rather than by leopards. I recognised Indian cheetahs when I saw them, of course? What had Titian been thinking?[12] Those colours, though, like nothing else in the world . . .

I could not listen to it and rushed out into Trafalgar Square, with Freddy at my heels, begging to know what he had said or done to offend me. He offered to do anything in the world to make amends, and I suggested we walk to New Bond Street and look at some jewellery.

I am not much for walks in London, but I felt shopping might restore my spirits. I was wearing a smart new *tailleur* in black and white, with a small black hat and white gloves, and my shoes were black slingback, peep-toe courts, quite suitable for walking. Freddy darted into a florist shop and came out with a blood-red camellia, which was just what the outfit needed to perk it up, and I marched down Regent Street and through the Burlington Arcade on the arm of a handsome young man who, truth be told, did not look quite English. I smiled and nodded to passers-by, graciously, like a Queen. A crowd began to follow us, and we were photographed entering Asprey's together. The English papers were still respecting the King's privacy, but a Protestant church weekly in Glasgow ran the picture with the headline, 'Something should be done!'

Ribbentrop kept up with the flowers and I kept gadding about with Freddy and people talked: was the godlike youth my *amant de coeur* or was he loyally distracting attention from his boss? With the addition of the camellia, though I had not realised it, I was sporting Nazi colours, black, white, and red. Queen Mary was furious and Cookie flew to Sandringham to egg her on, and the boy had a disagreeable hour on the telephone, as his mother told him what he must and must not do and how very, very deeply he had disappointed her. He told me everything she said, repeating it over and over, until I got tired of listening.

Lindbergh was out and about in England too, and Ribbentrop kept busy scraping acquaintance with lots of influential people. The King visited his mother hoping to sweeten her about our marriage. I always thought it was hopeless, but he thought, as he

Chapter Five

said each time he set off to see her, that she might be a little fond of him and want him to be happy. Whenever he was away, Nicolson and Duff or sometimes Somerset Maugham would drop in for KTs in the late afternoon. They were most attentive to me, really. Nicolson loathed Lindbergh. 'It's always a mistake for a woman to marry down, whatever neo-romantic Chatterley rubbish may be in the air. Lindbergh's essentially a mechanic,[13] with virtually no formal education.'

'Wasn't his father a Congressman?' Duff asked.

'For a time, some Midwestern crank. There are men in Congress the Labour Party would not nominate for our most blighted slum. Like his father, Lindbergh is full of intellectual enthusiasms. He's dabbling now in eugenics, immortality, and the occult.[14] Like most imperfectly educated men, he has no sense of his own limitations. People admire his feats of derring-do, and he's been flattered to the verge of madness.'

'Must be ghastly for his wife,' Duff said. 'He is appalling, but do you seriously believe that Lindbergh wants to make himself a dictator?'

'Roosevelt can manage worse than Lindbergh,' Nicolson said. 'It's England that must be put in safer hands. Your appearance on New Bond Street was inspired, my dear,' he said. 'Your idea or the graf's?'

'Mine,' I said. 'But he added the red camellia.'

'Stirred the Labour Party's Nonconformist depths,' Duff said. 'They've forgotten all about his trip to Wales.'

We were having drinks in the charming sitting room of my new house on Cumberland Terrace near Regent's Park[15] where I moved after Ernest left me. Security precautions required for a monarch's visits were easier to arrange in a house than a flat, and I was happy for the additional storage space. My wardrobe was outgrowing the flat at Bryanston Court, and I finally had enough space for my hats and my shoes.

In fact, my life suited me. 'I am having a lot of fun,' I said. 'And the King is not the least like Lindbergh. Do you really think he has to abdicate?'

'Absolutely. We are a deferential people,' Nicolson said. 'He could be made into something very dangerous indeed.'

'By the way,' Duff said, 'when you were at Asprey's, did you let the *graf* buy you some compromising trinket?'

'No, I bought seventeen sterling silver bud vases and had them send the bill to Ribbentrop.'

Chapter Six

Nicolson said I had done well and nothing remained to be done with Freddy or with Ribbentrop. I had established myself as a bad influence on the King, a silly woman who consorted with foreigners and who did not care enough about him even to preserve appearances. Now we needed to move quickly on the divorce and the abdication. He found me a barrister, Norman Birkett, KC,[1] one of the best, if not the best. There was nothing he could not say with a straight face. Several notorious criminals were free men because of his brilliant work. Birkett was expensive and worth every penny, and he found out that the fastest divorce in England was to be had in the county of Suffolk.

Sad to say, the petitioner had to live there. I'd been through that once already in Virginia, where I'd spent months in a dingy hotel having meals with Rotarians and travelling salesmen, a sleazy bunch but not one of them as slimy as Ribbentrop, in order to get rid of Win Spencer. This time I had to go to Felixstowe on the North Sea in October. Willie Maugham promised he'd stop by from time to time to buck me up. When he saw the place, which was awful, he called it Felixculpa, which he explained was a happy or a fortunate sin.

I had to dress badly in grey or beige tweeds. Plain black was permitted, of course, so I placed a somewhat frantic call to Coco Chanel for some of her smart little dresses. The barrister positively forbade me to wear fur, not even my foxes, and insisted on plain felt hats. No jewellery at all, no rings.

'I'm not divorced yet.'

'*De facto*, not yet *de jure*,' Birkett said grimly. He was something of a bully, but he had none of the charm that masterful men often have. It's a fine line. He was demanding and coached me very hard.

'No jewellery,' he went on. 'When you learned of your husband's treachery, you removed your wedding band. You could not bear to wear the symbol of the sacred bond he had profaned.'

'We were married at a registry.'

'The sacred token of your holy bond. Are you listening, Mrs Simpson?'

'Yes, the holy bond's sacred token.'

'That'll do. Fine, sacred token of your holy bond.'

'What about earrings?'

'Plain pearl, if you must, and no furs. Did I emphasise that sufficiently? There is something lascivious about animal skins, and some people see them as a vestige of savagery.'

'Yes,' I said. 'Some do. What about a veil?'

'No, you aren't a widow and you have nothing to hide. No make-up.'

Fool, I thought. No make-up he could see. As if I could appear in public in black or taupe without make-up.

So there I was, alone, in a dreary provincial town. The King's position was that I was free to do what I believed was right and that he would not presume to influence any friend on so personal a matter. He called me every night to complain about his mother's coldness and to repeat the nasty things she said to him. He repeated them over and over and I felt sorry for him.

I spent several weeks in Felixstowe, dressed in beige and grey and black, seeing the same colours in the dull sea and the dirty sand and the cloudy sky. Clouds were mostly grey and sometimes black, and it gets dark about two in the afternoon in the fall when you are that far north. The colours all around me looked as miserable as I felt myself.

Maugham came to see me and we walked along the harbour, nothing like Rhodes or Alexandria. I was very low.

' "Distant northern sea",' he said. 'Makes everyone sad.'

'Did you write that?' It sounded like he was quoting something.

Chapter Six

'No, but I feel it. It's very different from the Aegean that the other chap was thinking about, or the Mediterranean.'

'Yes.'

'This will pass. Everything does, you know.'

'I know that things don't last.'

'Like this frightful bondage to Simpson, dear heart. That will soon be over, and there will be brighter skies and far brighter seas.'

I gave my testimony. The manager testified. The room clerk testified. The barman testified. The girl who brought the breakfast trolley to Ernest and Buttercup Kennedy testified, though because of her extreme youth, Birkett handled her gently. 'You assumed the lady and gentleman whose breakfast you served were husband and wife, did you not, Miss Sprockett?'

'Oh, yes, sir, so I did, sir, they would of 'ad to be, wou'n' they, sir, or it would of been wrong for 'em to be cuddlin' like that, sir, in bed, sir, an 'er without a stitch.' Birkett handed the pudgy child down from the witness box like a princess from a carriage.

Last, he called the chambermaid. The judge cleared the court, myself included, and took evidence about the state of the bed linen. Birkett was thorough. Judges had become so familiar with this ploy, one member of an unhappy couple going to a hotel and being photographed with a third party, that they would sometimes get huffy and refuse to grant the divorce.

As it was, it still took some eloquence to get the decree nisi, which was granted, as the world knows, on October 27, 1936. The hitch was that the divorce did not become final for six months, but as long as I behaved myself, and in particular as long as I was not seen with the King – rumours of our friendship were now so public that a judge would have to take notice – I would be a free woman in the spring. Birkett was most emphatic about this. I must live like a nun. The King and I could not be seen together. It would be best if I went abroad. That suited me.

Birkett prided himself on getting the judge, despite his sarcasm and suspicion, to assign costs to the respondent. That sort of put the icing on the cake of me being the injured party, 'the blameless and broken-hearted victim of her beloved husband's lust and perfidy,' said with a straight face. Ernest had to pay for the whole thing, and he refused to be reimbursed, people told me. I must say, he behaved awfully well. I believe he wanted me to be free to marry the King.

Willie drove me back to London, and I felt my spirits reviving. News hawkers were out with the evening papers, shouting something about the Huns and the Eyeties, but I could not make out the rest of it.

Nicolson and Duff Cooper were at my house when we arrived. 'The fat's in the fire. Ciano's been in Berlin less than a week, and a treaty was signed today.'[2]

'*Felix culpa*,' Duff said. 'You got it right, old boy. It's providential. Edward VIII will be gone not a moment too soon.'

'The Count was in Berlin while I was in Felixstowe?'

'Just a few days, apparently, so far as anyone knows. There cannot have been much to discuss. No language to iron out. The Austrians were nowhere to be seen and it appears that the Tyrol was not discussed, not at any length, at any rate. Nor the Balkans. They'll divvy up the spoils later.'

'What does this mean?' I asked.

'It means that our debt to you, dear lady,' Nicolson said, 'is beyond measure. Of World Historic Importance.' His words sounded sometimes like he spoke them in capital letters.

Duff said, 'I will find a way to thank you, to acknowledge your sacrifice, not in any obvious way, but so that those who care to know will know.'

I simply could not believe my ears. 'He hates the Germans.'

'I expect he does what he's told.' Nicolson was grim.

'He can't have been there and not . . . I mean, Berlin's so close to where I was staying on the coast. Not more than a few hours by plane.'

'Quite.' 'That's the point.' 'Exactly.' They all spoke at once.

'What does this mean?' I repeated. 'Will somebody please tell me what this means for me?'

'Give us a minute,' Maugham said, 'and bring us some gin.' He took me into the kitchen, which was empty of servants because they all ate their heads off when I was away.[3] I could not afford to keep them on board wages, so I sent them off on holiday, except for my maid, who came with me to Felixstowe.

We sat at the kitchen table and he poured some gin into a teacup. 'Drink this.'

I drank it and he poured some more.

'You must not blame yourself,' he said. 'I was sent to Russia to prevent the Bolshevik revolution.[4] No one succeeds every time. You must not take it personally.'

'I don't care about politics.'

'I understand,' he said, and I believed him. 'It was probably inevitable that Hitler and Mussolini would agree to work in concert. The Count, whatever his private thoughts, could most likely not have prevented it. The King's pro-German. You'll be seeing more of Count Ciano now than otherwise.'

'You promised me that when I was finished in Felixstowe, I could go to Italy. That I had to leave England. "Brighter skies", you said, "and far brighter seas".'

'That is off, for the moment, I am afraid, but you could go to Nice. I have a villa at Cap Ferrat. You could visit me.'

'All of you led me on. You said I would have six months entirely to myself. Nicolson was talking about how early in the spring wildflowers bloom in Sicily.'

I had never drunk gin straight before and I was feeling rather weepy. He gave me some more.

'You'll be able to sleep now. Everything will look better tomorrow. The Count's dealings with Hitler need not affect his feelings for you.'

My maid had come back by train with the luggage and she helped me undress and get into bed. I felt woozy, but I could hear the three of them talking.

'On such a day,' Nicolson was saying, 'the King of England called this house fifteen times between the hours of four and five-thirty in the afternoon. When Hitler and Mussolini have agreed to make war on all we cherish, on all that he ought to hold dearer than life.'

'If it's war on all he holds dear,' Duff Cooper said, 'my money's on Italy. Meeting Ciano was a *coup de foudre*. It surprised me, because I thought she was as hard as nails.'[5]

'You're sure it's the first time they've met?' Nicolson asked. 'There is all that talk about China.'

'*Colpo di fulmine*,' Maugham said. 'I agree with Duff. She cannot have known him long. She was mooning about him all the time we were in Egypt.'

'God.' Nicolson's voice. Very bitter. 'The King's such a mutt. Makes a man yearn for Cromwell.'

'We don't need Cromwell, old boy,' Duff said. 'We have Mrs Simpson.'

The phone rang and my maid answered it. 'The King, ma'am, he's been calling.'

'Give him to Mr Maugham. I'm not feeling well. Bring him in here. I want to listen.'

Willie took the call in my bedroom. 'Maugham here, Your Majesty. No, sir, I regret that Mrs Simpson cannot come to the telephone. She was magnificent in Felixstowe, if you will grant me the liberty of speaking so personally, but she became utterly unstrung when Birkett told her that she must not be seen with you for six months. She went completely to pieces after all she'd been through. We had to have a doctor, sir, to give her something to help her sleep.' There was a pause. 'Her maid's with her, sir. Worships her as we all do and says it would be a sin to wake her. I assure you it

     Chapter Six

would be worth my life to try.' Another pause. 'Yes, she inspires passionate love and loyalty.' A longer pause, and Willie said, 'Certainly, I will. Of course, Sire, anything you wish. I am yours to command.

'The King's not a great reader,' Willie said after he put down the telephone. 'But he knows me by reputation. He begged me to stay with you until you awoke.'

Chapter Seven

I decided to stay in England for the time being. There wasn't anywhere else I could go where I wanted to be and the King needed a lot of looking after, which all had to be done in private so it did not jeopardise my divorce. This kept me indoors for all the short days and long nights, the very long nights, of November in England, some of the time in London, most of the time at Fort Belvedere, the King's country getaway at Windsor. The Fort, he called it. He had many official duties to perform, and all of them were boring and tiresome and took his time away from things he liked to do. He had to lay a wreath on Armistice Day in memory of the soldiers who died in the Great War. He had to open Parliament and read a speech about what the Government was going to do next, and he made another trip to Wales, where he found more miners out of work. All these burdens put him in low spirits and he played the bagpipes before and after dinner. That generally cheered him. It did nothing for me.

I can remember only two outings during that whole dreary month that gave me any pleasure. I had a very nice day, after Queen Mary left Buckingham Palace, going through the place with Elsie Mendl[1] and planning how I could redo it completely and make it really smart and elegant. But that, alas, was not to be. Another day, I took Anne Lindbergh shopping. She was a sad, timid little thing, and I think she was the only good woman who ever really admired me. When she told me how beautiful I always looked and how difficult she found it to dress well, I took pity on her. I helped her choose some nice outfits for the winter – little did I know she was pregnant at the time and they would all go to waste – and after we finished shopping, I took her to tea at Claridge's.

Chapter Seven

She began to talk about Germany, where she went with her husband and where women, she told me, looking terribly unhappy and worried, were not respected as we ought to be. It was frightful, she said. German women didn't seem to dare to express political opinions and yet political prejudices kept them from finding inspiration and solace in literature as women in other civilised countries always do. Nobody would discuss Rilke with her.[2] They thought he was a degenerate. 'Isn't that sad, Mrs Simpson? Could you live without literature?'

'Who could?' I'd never heard of Rilke, who, I suppose, like a lot of writers, was either a Jew or a pansy, or both.

Then, out of the blue, she asked, 'You met President Atatürk on your cruise?'

'We did.'

'And many other important and influential persons?'

'Several.'

'Did you have a chance to talk with any of them about the emancipation of women?'

Her question floored me. Memories came rushing back, memories that had nothing to do with emancipation. I finally managed to say I hadn't.

'Dear Mrs Simpson,' she said. 'I am so sorry if I distressed you. I know how difficult it can be to try and help men see reason, but we must be patient and gentle, mustn't we? And firm, and surely, in time, reasonable men will understand that we have minds and souls as they do.'

'My meetings weren't so bad, all in all.' Minds and souls, imagine! If I were married to Charles Lindbergh, the only thing I'd want him to know I had was a lawyer. A good one, like Norman Birkett, KC.

'I'm so happy to hear that,' she said. 'I get discouraged sometimes. May we see the sweets trolley now?'

The poor child chose an eclair and a meringue and she enjoyed them. While she was cleaning her plate of whipped cream and chocolate glaze, I asked her to tell me more about Germany and the people she met there. She said they had not met Hitler and they didn't know Göbbels and his wife very well. The Göbbelses were special friends, as I'd probably heard, of Sir Oswald and Diana Mosley, and she thought that Germans who knew an Englishwoman as divinely glamorous and beautiful as Lady Mosley wouldn't care about a plain little American like her. The couple she knew best, because of her husband's interest in aviation, were the Görings. 'There was a map with parts of France and Poland the same colour as Germany, in a lighter shade'[3] – she leaned across the table, speaking very low –'but Charles says lots of Germans live in those territories.'

'What are they like as people?' I was curious about them because I'd heard that Göring and Ribbentrop didn't like each other.

Frau Göring was Nordic-looking, she said, with 'corn-blond hair,' and perhaps the tiniest little bit overdressed. She'd entertained them at lunch in a floor-length green velvet gown with an emerald and diamond swastika brooch. About the man, she said he made her uncomfortable, an 'inflated Alcibiades'[4] she called him. I don't know who Alcibiades is, but I gathered she disapproved of Göring. Her hubby would scold her, I feared, if he caught her talking about the new Germany the way she described it to me.

Those outings, with Elsie and with little Mrs Lindbergh, were my two flings in the month after I left Felixstowe. I couldn't even see Freddy because Duff thought there were people in the German embassy who would block the divorce if they could. Here I was, the *femme fatale* all the world was talking about, making no whoopee at all. A scarlet woman serenaded by bagpipes.

The King became more and more blue. He felt hounded, he said, on all sides, and friendless. It wasn't easy to keep him focused on what he needed to do, but in the end he summoned the Prime Minister and told him he was going to marry me and that was that and he could like it or lump it. The Prime Minister did not like it and, as for lumping it, he would have to consult the Cabinet and the House of Commons.[5] The King was firm for a day or two and the Prime Minister said he must consult the Dominions also. The King was leaning to the morganatic marriage plan that Nicolson had specifically warned me to resist, the 'sordid half measure.' The publisher of the *Daily Mail* took me to lunch at Claridge's to explain what a good plan it was.[6] There were people, it seemed, who wanted the boy to remain on the throne.

A morganatic marriage was easier talked about than done. England had never had one and it turned out to be such an innovation that Parliament couldn't do it on its own, even if it wanted to, which it didn't. The Dominions, or most of them, would have to agree.

The poor boy asked Duff Cooper – he trusted him as a friend – to luncheon to talk about the Dominions.[7] Duff told me he tried to make him see it was impossible. The Australians are prudish, as middle-class folk generally are, and the new Governor General of Canada, Lord Tweedsmuir, was, I think Duff said, *obdurate*. 'Tweedsmuir's a son of the manse,' he explained.

'What's a manse?' I asked.

'The home of a Scottish clergyman.'

'How did this man get to be a peer and Governor General of Canada if his father was only a preacher?' I suspected he might be a pal of Cookie's. I was not fond of Scotland and I always felt it was mutual.

'Hard work,' [8] Duff said.

Duff came to see me often in those days, sometimes with Nicolson, sometimes with Willie Maugham, and one day they all came together. 'You will have to go abroad as soon as possible.' I don't remember who spoke first, but it was a united front. 'The King must abdicate before the New Year, and if you leave England, that will frighten him into action.'

'What's the rush?'

'It's getting ugly at home and dangerous abroad. The British

Union of Fascists is demonstrating in favour of the marriage. Three thousand people came to a rally bellowing "Long live the King and long live Bessie".'

'Bessie?' I was never baptised, as King George and Queen Mary supposedly found out in their research on my past, but I always said I was christened Bessie Wallis Warfield, with family names as is customary in the South. I didn't like the name Bessie and never used it. 'Who's calling me Bessie?'

'Oswald Mosley. "Bessie" makes you more human and more English. He's demanding a referendum on the marriage issue.[9] There have been scuffles. People could get hurt.'

'Baldwin may resign and force an election.'

I thought that might not be such a bad thing, and Nicolson reminded me of the tragedy so narrowly averted in July.

'You've had death threats yourself, have you not?'

'Not any I took seriously. Cranks.'

'Cranks – who else?' Duff said. 'What do you expect assassins to be? Choirboys?'

He had a point.

'But quite apart from civil disturbances, there are foreign issues to consider. There really is a great deal at stake, Wallis,' Duff said, and I think that was the first time he called me by my name. Diana Cooper did almost from the first, but he was more formal. Old school. 'Asia is in play now. Germany and Japan signed an Anti-Comintern Pact this morning. And touching on the East, haven't your friends the Rogerses, the people you stopped with in Peking, invited you to France? Hasn't Rogers come to England to fetch you?'

'He says Katherine's hurt I didn't come right after Felixstowe. What's a Comintern?'

'The Communist International – Russia, in plain English.'

'The King will like that. You know what he thinks of Bolshevism.'

'You invariably grasp the nettle,' Willie said.

'There is going to be a world war,' Duff said, 'and soon.'

'Which brings us, my dear, to the subject of China.' Nicolson picked up where Duff left off.

'I thought this was about Japan.'

'Right again, but China and Japan are neighbours – not, alas, good neighbours. Your friends the Rogerses have many friends there.'

They certainly did. All sorts.

'I wondered,' Maugham said, 'just on the off chance that the subject of China may have come up during your delightful visit to Rhodes, did Count Ciano ever speak to you of Madame Chiang Kai-shek?'

'Oh, come,' Nicolson said. 'The Methodist bluestocking wife of a Chinese warlord? The man must be a satyr.'

Maugham shot him an angry glance and Duff shook his head.

'Count Ciano never spoke to me of any other woman,' I said. And he hadn't. Not his wife, not his mother, not his sister or his aunts, not the wives of brothers or friends, not his first love or any subsequent loves, not pretty girls he was too shy to talk to when he was a boy, not haughty beauties who scorned him when he was older. Not that I suppose any woman ever scorned him. Meanwhile, in England, the King's hurt feelings were getting on my nerves. 'Never.'

'I told you he's an intelligent man,' Duff said.

Maugham continued. 'This would have been strictly line of duty. I'm sure she isn't his type at all. But this is important, old girl. He was posted there in the twenties and Mussolini sent him back right after his marriage. Chiang Kai-shek admires the Fascists and he's already dealt with Ciano.'[10]

Oriental women were irresistible, exotic doormats. I'd seen it time and time again. And was there any woman who wasn't his type?

'You had Peking and Shanghai in common,' Duff said. 'Did you never swap stories, as two old China hands?'

'We didn't talk very much, actually.'

'His English is excellent,' Duff said, and he and Diana did seem to have a lot to say to each other, every single day. Some couples do.

'Why is this so important?'

'We think,' Duff said, 'they, the Germans and the Japanese, may offer Chiang a deal. That they want to make use of him the way they want to make use of the King, to confuse people and divide their loyalties. If he co-operates, they'll leave him in nominal control of China. He can continue to slaughter his own Communists and Japanese troops will be free to attack the Soviets from Manchuria. Germany has no history with China and the Italians have been there for years and Ciano recently.'

'Why does Chiang's wife matter? Is he uxorious?'

'Flagrantly unfaithful, from all account,' Maugham said. 'But he knows no Western languages and he relies on her knowledge and judgment of foreigners in his dealings with Europeans.'

'Unlike that cretin Lindbergh, Chiang has the brains to value an intelligent and perceptive woman.' For a man of his tastes, Nicolson seemed strangely taken with Anne Lindbergh.

'If she likes Ciano,' Duff said, 'if there's some history, we need to know.'

'And whose daughter is she?'

'Her father was a Methodist missionary. She grew up in the States and went to Wellesley College.'

'Wellesley girl. Imagine that.' I remembered something. 'The Count asked me where I went to college.' He thought I must be awfully highbrow if I could quote poetry and not know common words like rooster or son-in-law.

'Go on,' Maugham said, and raised his hand for silence. The others should not interrupt. He must have known how to make people tell their stories.

'I told him only grubby frumps went to college.'[11]

'Quite.'

'He said something about good women and soup.'

'Yes.'

'He said that I was as learned as I was beautiful, and an American once told him their college did not, as you'd expect, produce only lesbians. They could also turn out loyal and reliable wives.'

' "Reliable"?'

'Yes, "reliable". And then he said something about soup.'

'They also cook, these paragons?'

'No, no, it was a particular kind of soup. Minestrone. He said it twice, "Minestrone, minestrone". I didn't quite catch it. He said it as if it had made an impression on him.' Gallo had been stark naked, feeding me figs, so I wasn't paying close attention to his words. Then he said education hadn't spoiled my enchanting femininity and conversation lagged.

Nicolson rose. 'We'll have to call Washington.'

The three of us chatted of this and that after he left. Duff asked where the Rogerses lived in France. It was near Cannes, was it not? House with some evocative Provençal name, Lou Viei? Maugham said I must come to him for Christmas. P. G. Wodehouse might be there. Duff said that would be delightful for me, and he himself would always rather be in France than anywhere else in the world.

'*Non ministrari sed ministrare*,' Nicolson said when he rejoined us. 'Motto of Wellesley College. "To serve rather than to be served".'

'Jolly good,' Duff said. ' "Not to be coddled but to act on one's own". Splendid. And conclusive, you agree?'

Duff rushed back to Whitehall and Nicolson went off to write an article and Maugham stayed with me. He told me a funny story to cheer me up. He said it was making the rounds in Washington and London. Roosevelt told Joseph Kennedy he'd like to make him ambassador to England, but ambassadors had to be presented to the King in court dress: puffy pantaloons and hose and low buckled shoes. His calves would have to cut the mustard or it was no go. He made Kennedy drop his trousers, in the White House, in front of a lot of foreign policy advisers, and they all agreed his legs were out of the question.[12]

'Everyone must be pleased he isn't coming,' I said, thinking Roosevelt must be better than people said, in spite of all the hardship caused by the New Deal.

Maugham shook his head. 'Roosevelt granted him a week to see if he could get permission to wear a morning coat. People say Kennedy's first call was Lindbergh, because he knows how things are done in England.'

Chapter Eight

On the night of December 1, there was a big fire in London. The Crystal Palace, built for some jamboree in Queen Victoria's day, burned to the ground.[1] The Victorian era was really over now, people said, and some people talked about the Wrath of God. A brick was thrown through my window the next day and the brick threw the King into a panic. He insisted that I leave England for a little while, until he could convince the Prime Minister and the Cabinet and the Dominions and the Archbishop of Canterbury and his Mother that I was the only girl in the world. He was still planning to delay his Coronation until my divorce became final so we could be married and crowned together.

It was decided that I would leave the Fort on the evening of December 3. Several cars would be sent out from various gates of Windsor Castle and Great Park, and then I would go, driven by the King's chauffeur, accompanied by Aunt Bessie, who'd come from America to chaperone me, Lord Perry Brownlow, an old friend of the boy's, and an inspector from Scotland Yard. Herman Rogers went back to Cannes to help Katherine prepare for my coming and protect against an onslaught of reporters.[2]

That afternoon, Nicolson came to see me to discuss what must be done with and about the King in the coming months. My divorce would not be final until April and I could not marry him and take charge in person until then. 'It is essential,' Nicolson said, 'that the public continue to believe you exercise some strange fascination over him.'

I didn't think that was a very nice way to put it. 'He's head over heels in love with me. Isn't that what I'm good for?'

'You must be seen to control him, to manipulate him. Being in love is sympathetic, being a chump is not.'

Nicolson dictated a number of what he called talking points for me to use when I called the King from France. I wrote them on scraps of paper. He said it must look as if I jotted these down in a hurry, desperate and playing for time, using some transparent alias, like Mr James for the Court of St. James.

The points were:

1) MR JAMES SHOULD NOT STEP DOWN. Which he was more and more eager to do. It had to look like I wanted him to remain King so that my lover would continue to be one of the most important men in the world and I was such a hussy that I did not care if he married me or not. That marriage meant nothing to me. Well, it didn't really. I never cared if married men I liked slept with their wives. I knew they had to do it every now and then.

2) HE SHOULD CONSULT BROADLY AND SEEK ADVICE FROM MANY PEOPLE – DUFF, LORD DERBY, THE AGA KHAN.[3]

'Why the Aga Khan?' That struck me as funny because it was the Aga Khan's dashing son, Aly Khan, who swept away the boy's previous favourite, Thelma Furness, and carried her off to Spain a year or so ago, leaving the field clear for me.

'A spiritual leader, venerated by millions in the Empire, from a religious tradition that permits divorce, embraces it, so to speak.'

'How about a rabbi?'

'We must not strain credulity, my dear. No one would believe the King cares about the Jews.'

'What's in this for the Aga Khan?'

'Very good.' He smiled as if I'd said something bright. A look I never saw on the face of a teacher. 'Since you ask, he's getting Partition.'

'Partition of what?'

'Of British India after the war, a separate Muslim state. There will be a frightful blood-bath, but we had to agree. The Germans are offering the Muslims all of India, as well as a free hand in Palestine, of course.'

'What about Kashmir?'

'We agreed to disagree. Now the next point:

3) DO NOTHING RASH. PUT EVERYTHING OFF FOR A YEAR. And, this is most important:

4) MAKE RADIO ADDRESS TO THE NATION EVEN IF CABINET REFUSES. Be sure you underscore the part about the Cabinet, two or three times.'

I had suggested that myself, weeks ago, but apparently the Sovereign may not speak on the wireless without the consent of his ministers. It is absolutely taboo. And the Brits make such a fuss about freedom of speech. Hypocrites, really.

I put the notes in my handbag and made sure they were there when I left after tea, after many hugs and kisses and much teary snivelling. We drove straight to Newhaven and caught the cross-Channel ferry. The British part went smoothly, packs of reporters following all the decoy cars as they dispersed to ports all over England. There were difficulties with the *douane* at Dieppe. I think the French wanted to make sure I was actually leaving England and had packed enough clothes for a long stay, which was stupid really, because how hard is it to buy clothes in France? That must have occurred to them, because they asked to see my jewellery too. We were in the customs shed for hours, and when they let us go, the press were in hot pursuit. I was exhausted and tried to sleep in the car, but I couldn't and I could not go another mile without a cup of tea.

We stopped at the Hôtellerie du Grand Cerf in Evreux, where I made a big fuss about needing to make an important phone call. The Scotland Yard fellow found the proprietor and he placed the call for me himself. I do not speak French well and I cannot speak it on the telephone. The *hôtelier* – I know the words for most important things, but I never learned the verbs – handed me the receiver, bowed from the waist, and stood very respectfully some distance away to protect my privacy. Gallant as he was, he was unable to do that. The connection was terrible and I was shouting, partly because the King could not hear me, partly because I wanted everyone in the inn to hear me, and partly because my nerves were a bit frazzled.[4]

We drove very fast through France. We stopped at Blois and then south of Lyon, where I had to escape from a three-star restaurant through a kitchen window, and arrived finally at Cannes, three days after I left Windsor. I had to crouch down on the floor in the back seat with a blanket over my head as the car swept through the gates of the Rogerses' villa.

I called Nicolson on a much better line as soon as I got inside.

'You left the notes?'

'Yes, at a charming inn in Evreux. Proprietor was an angel.'

'That must be the reason.'

'Reason for what?'

'Not a whisper about them in the press. Proprietor of a place like that's likely to be a royalist with crypto-Fascist sympathies. He probably found them and put them in a safe place. You should have gone to a café. The owner would have been a Radical, possibly even a Freemason.'

I lost my temper. 'Maybe I should have asked him his opinions about the war in Spain. You told me to leave them as soon as I saw the press was on to me.'

He apologised nicely. 'We may not need them, in any case. Things are shaping nicely here. We'll have the King in the bank by New Year's. I'll fetch the notes if you like, when things cool down.'[5]

I more or less collapsed into a hot bath and the Rogerses had meals served to me in bed for several days. When I had not been seen outdoors for a week, some evil person, and I do not know to this day

Chapter Eight

who it was, sent a doctor, an obstetrician, with an anesthesiologist from London. If I needed their attention, needless to say, I hadn't been living like a nun since my wicked husband deserted me, and I wouldn't get my divorce. Herman threw them off the grounds and began to sleep, or so he said, with a pistol under his pillow.[6]

In addition to the doctor and his assistant and hordes of photographers, dozens of other people wanted to scrape acquaintance. I had been in France less than a week when a man called Charles Bedaux[7] wrote offering me the use of his château. He described it, the Château de Candé, as an ancestral property always ready to shelter damsels in distress. I was, of course, no damsel, and he was not what he pretended to be either. Herman told me he was some sort of guttersnipe who left France as a lad, a step ahead of the police or the mob or both, and made a fortune in America making people in factories work harder by taking moving pictures of them. Nicolson said he was perfect, one could not have made him up, and Duff said to be careful, 'He's *louche* and the perfect *entrée* into a rather bad lot of French people.' Duff Cooper loved France and the existence of people like that pained him. 'Do not think for one moment that men like Bedaux speak for *la France profonde*.' I had no idea what that was, but I promised Duff I wouldn't. 'You may want to take him up on his offer at some point, but for the moment, tell him your plans are not settled.'

It turned out, sooner than I expected, that the King really couldn't live without me. Duff and the others who'd known him longer than I had predicted it would happen before the end of the year. There were news reports that he tried to drink himself to death and his valet found him unconscious and that he revived only after they pumped his stomach.[8] I never asked him if that was a true story. I thought it would be tactless. Anyway, a few days after I left, he met with his mother and his brothers and told them he was going to abdicate. The Articles of Abdication were going to be signed on

December 10, and Duff told me that after, and only after, he had signed them and York had been proclaimed King George VI would the poor fellow be permitted to go on the radio. Winston Churchill was writing the speech, and it was just what the occasion required. I could see it now: Mr and Mrs Temple, and Shirley Temple and little Rosie Temple all waving from the Palace balcony, and Cookie in particular pleased as punch. 'He's going to be called the Duke of Windsor,' Duff said, 'and we'll have him safe in the bank before Christmas.'

Nicolson had used that expression too, 'in the bank'.

'Why do you say "in the bank"? Where is he going?'

'My dear, such things cannot be discussed over the telephone. You'll know soon enough.'

'It isn't too bourgeois?'

'By no means. And his hostess is delightful, a woman of infinite resource and sagacity.'

'Pretty?' I did not like the sound of a delightful hostess.

'Handsome, rather.'

'How old is she?'

'Of a certain age.'

'In years.' Some people would have described me as a woman of a certain age. In the States, close to forty, I would be 'on the shelf'.[9]

'Fiftyish, no less. She is not a flirt, my dear, she is *sérieuse*, and she knows better than most what's at stake.'

Three days later, no longer King of England, the boy was delivered to Schloss Enzesfeld, the seat of the Austrian Rothschilds, and into the care of Baroness Eugène de Rothschild, formerly Kitty Wolf of Philadelphia.[10]

Chapter Nine

Baroness Rothschild made her guest go to church on Christmas Eve. 'If you want peace so much,' she told him, as he reported in a long, cross letter, 'go and pray for it.' On Christmas Eve, I went with Willie Maugham to the Casino,[1] wearing a red silk organza dress. He put some ivy in my hair, which he said was traditional for English brides and added a seasonal note to my scarlet woman costume. My engagement ring, a huge Moghul emerald,[2] was green too, so I had a sort of a holly-and-ivy look, and I was ready for any kind of celebration.

We got back to the villa around three in the morning, after drinking gallons of champagne, and found a courier waiting – he'd been ordered to put the package into my hands – with my Christmas present from my fiancé. I opened it and found, inside a suede Hermès *pochette*, a solid gold powder compact. One side was gem-studded, lots and lots of precious stones, all large and nicely arranged, and on the other side the silly boy had them do the itinerary of our cruise, mapped out in black and red enamel.[3] Rhodes wasn't there. Or Alexandria. I stared at the map and kept turning the compact over and over – I remember being agitated and I believe I raised my voice – looking for something that wasn't there. 'Where's Rhodes? Oh, God, what has the ninny done with Rhodes? Why can't I ever, ever in my life, get what I want?'

I must have been very drunk and Willie, who was none too sober himself, bent down and picked up an envelope. 'This fell out when you tore the package open. Shall I read it?'

'Sure,' I said. 'Why not?' I tried to pull myself together.

' "My own . . . ." I will skip the salutation. I am skipping also the doggie kisses from the Cairn terriers. Here, I think, is the pith: "I had them make our cruise perfect. No engine conking. No horrid toothache. Perfect the way our life will be forever after . . . " I'll omit the closing also.'

It finally hit me. What it was going to be like being married to a child of forty. And of fifty, and very likely of sixty. I didn't cry. I picked up a heavy crystal ashtray from the table in front of the sofa and threw it as hard as I could so that it smashed on the hearth.

'You've saved the world, don't you know? You may have averted a world war. If England and France hold tight, you should be able to go anywhere you like once you're married.' He was holding the boy's note in his hand and rereading it. 'You could probably invite other friends to join you on your honeymoon. He's not likely to object.'

I collapsed onto the sofa with my head in my hands. I felt very sick. I didn't have the energy to throw anything else. Willie sat down beside me. 'Want a nightcap? No? I don't want one either. Look here, there's another envelope on the table addressed to you. Shall I open it?'

'Where's it from?'

'The States. I'm sorry, my dear. You *are* famous,' he said. 'It's a Christmas card from Mae West.[4] I'd give anything to have one.'

I had a lot to drink and didn't wake up until late in the afternoon on Christmas Day. It was raining. Even on the Riviera, winter days can be dull. When I went downstairs, Willie and another man were sitting by a blazing fire reading from typewritten sheets. All the broken glass had been swept from the hearth and the card from Mae West was propped up against a vase of red roses that were wilting in the heat of the fire.

'Good morning, my dear. Merry Christmas.' Willie rose. 'Yes, there are seventeen flowers. A bounder called Bedaux brought them, a tribute from a mutual friend on this holy day. I told him you'd risen early and gone out with your maid to distribute alms. I did not encourage him to wait.'

'Thanks,' I said. 'Merry Christmas to you, too.'

'This is Plum.' It was his friend, the writer P. G. Wodehouse. 'We are reading each other's works in progress. What can we get for you? Breakfast? Tea? A glass of wine? You're not quite ready for Christmas dinner, are you?'

I had a bit of dry toast and some tea, and while I breakfasted, Plum Wodehouse began to read aloud a story about a dim-witted young man with an aunt who made his life a living hell. The more he read, the more it sounded like the boy's troubles with his mother.

'I've used "hopeless imbecile" and "drivelling half-wit" and "dithering invertebrate" countless times. I need something fresh. What would a high-born old lady call a young relative who constantly mortified and disappointed her?'

I'd heard all the nasty things Queen Mary said so often I'd memorised them. I felt sorry for the boy. She was his mother, after all. ' "You are a canker on the rose of England",' I said. ' "I say *canker* because you do not have the gumption of the average beetle or the tenacity of an aphid".' There was a rose garden named after her in Regent's Park near my house in Cumberland Terrace. I made a point of never going there. ' "Or the discretion of the dimmest snail".'

'Garden image is good,' Wodehouse said. 'Very good. But I need something shorter here.'

' "Feckless drone", "Vapid and frivolous wastrel", ' I said, sipping tea and feeling a bit stronger.

'Jolly good. "Vapid and frivolous wastrel" it is.'

Maugham smiled. 'So art does imitate nature after all, rather than the other way round.'

I made a vow on Christmas Day 1936 that I would not just fade away into spas and casinos with a vapid wastrel. I would not turn into a pathetic has-been. Half the women who picked up pins in Coco Chanel's fitting rooms claimed they'd danced with the Tsar. I would make sure I had all the money I needed and the title I had earned, Her Royal Highness, the Duchess of Windsor. I knew Cookie would deny me the extra *chic* of the HRH if she could.[5]

I was pleased, the first week in January, to find that I had been chosen 'Woman of the Year' by *Time* magazine. Polly Whitman and about a hundred other people sent it to me. The portrait on the cover was reasonably flattering. The article was catty. Like a lot of others, it said how ordinary I was and how strange it was that so many men over so many years enjoyed my company, and that I treated the King badly, called him Boysy and generally ordered him around, but he didn't seem to mind. It quoted the Archbishop of York's helpful advice that men should steer clear of other men's wives before passion overcame them and they yielded to temptation they should have avoided in the first place. No wonder he rose so high in the Church of England.

I was curious about this honour because I never read news-magazines and I asked Willie Maugham who was *Time*'s 'Woman of the Year' last year. Imagine my surprise when he told me they'd never had a woman before, only men. 'If memory serves,' Willie said, 'the first was Charles Lindbergh, and you're certainly an improvement over him.'

'Who was it last year?'

'Haile Selassie, as a matter of fact.' He began to chuckle. 'Funny, isn't it? Mussolini must be wondering when it will be his turn.'

I kept track after that and the next year they chose Generalissimo and Mme Chiang Kai-shek.[6] She looked a fright, not even a *belle laide*.

Weeks passed, and it became clear to me that the 'Woman of the Year' would have to take charge of 'Boysy' and make him take a strong line with his family. Present a series of demands, or else. I hadn't settled then on what the 'or else' would be, but I was sure I'd think of something. I was absolutely clear about the minimum we had to have: Our engagement and our marriage must be

Chapter Nine

announced in the Court Circular and the King must attend our wedding. If his mother and Cookie did not let him come himself, then at least the younger Royals, his sister and brothers, must be present, and Dicky and Edwina Mountbatten, and a good showing of the smart set. An income suitable for our position, capital settled absolutely, not an allowance dribbling in with conditions attached. But above all and not negotiable: I had to have the title 'Her Royal Highness'.

The greatest lover in the history of the world was moping at Enzesfeld, designing monograms for the notepaper we would use after we were married. He kept calling to ask if the crown should be large or small and if it should be set over or beneath our intertwined initials. He'd noticed some time ago that our initials, W and E, spelled WE [7] – or EW, it could be that too, but he thought it should be WE and a sign that Heaven meant us to be together. He wrote long letters too almost every day, about how hard it was to wait and how much he missed me. He was a great one for *billets-doux*. Even if we were in the same house and, for whatever reason, sleeping in different rooms, I would find a note on my breakfast tray about how he could never go to sleep –'drowsels' he called it – without me. I could tell he was unhappy and getting desperate.

Towards the end of January, Kitty Rothschild called. We wrote and spoke fairly often and, as Americans, we understood each other. 'Wallis,' she said. 'I felt you should hear this first from me. I had to lock him in his room.' She went on to explain that he seemed at loose ends, so they'd taken him for a special treat to the opera in Vienna. *The Magic Flute*. She thought he would like it. She had never known anyone not to like it, *jamais de la vie*, but he didn't. He complained a good deal, people shushed him, and they had to take him home after the first act.

That gave me a pang. 'He doesn't care for opera.'

'Evidently not. When we got him home, he announced that he needed more exercise. He wanted to leave at first light for a ski resort on the German frontier and my husband and I concluded that he was planning to bolt. There was really nothing else to do.'

'It was the right thing to do.'

'I am so glad you agree. If he were my son – ' she went on. Kitty was about ten years older than the boy, not more. ' – I would ship him off to a kibbutz.' She explained that these were communal farms in Palestine that she and her husband supported where young people who'd been pampered and sheltered all their lives did very well digging irrigation ditches and planting orange trees. 'I do not say that hard physical labour is all he needs, but it would be a start.'

'You don't really think he should go to Palestine now, do you?'

'Heavens no. Somebody would shoot him in the first fifteen minutes and blame everyone else and all hell would break loose. I admire Queen Mary, Wallis, I really do, however unkind her behaviour may seem to you. Mothers do what they need to do,' Kitty Rothschild said rather grimly, and then she said something about Rebecca in the Bible that I did not follow. 'Honestly, I would not be in your shoes for all the tea in China. I don't know how we shall ever be able to express our gratitude.'

She watched him like a hawk after that and he complained about how she never left him alone and how stupid and tactless she was and I had to pretend that I was jealous and chalk it all up to his 'fatal charm'.

Finally, I put it to him:

Dear Lightning Brain [I wrote on February 6, 1937[8]] I must advise writing to your brother instead of the telephone. I think that with a slow brain such as his that he doesn't take in ideas as quickly as you speak and then the constant yelling which one has to do is apt to get on the nerves of a highly strung person. I know it's hard for you to write but feel that at this critical time in our lives you must make every effort and force yourself to do unpleasant tasks . . .

I had to make him take a stand. I had to make him believe, against

Chapter Nine

all the evidence, that he was a virile and masterful man, irresistible to Kitty Wolf, a tough customer. She had already ditched one pathetic nobleman, an Austrian count, to marry a Rothschild.[9] 'I can only pray to God that in your loneliness you haven't flirted with her.'

It was not subtle, but it worked, and finally in April he screwed up his courage and promised to write to his brother. He wrote first to me:

2. iv. 37 . . . I will be drafting a good letter and send it at a spycological [sic] moment embodying all your points which are flawless.[10]

By then, I was a wreck, living like a nun and waiting for the man who had given up everything to do something. I came very close myself to ditching the whole thing and going home to Baltimore. Charles Bedaux had been very persistent and attentive ever since I arrived in France, and in the end he positively forced his château on me. I took up residence in the Château de Candé in March, and it was a scary place. It was the first and only time in all those years that I felt I was in physical danger. The day after I got there, I took my dog for a walk and he ran off, out of the garden and into the park. A few minutes later, he let out the most blood-curdling howl and he died an hour or so later.

The Duke of Windsor was prostrated with grief and insisted that I have the poor precious embalmed. He ordered a little lead casket and made arrangements for the remains to be shipped to England and buried at Windsor. His brother, the King, he said, quite understood his feelings in this crisis, as he failed to do in other crises, and offered all the sympathy he could hope for and promised to find the animal a proper resting place in the royal park.

The vet told me that the cause of death was definitely snakebite and that the snake was, most likely, a viper.[11] I called Willie Maugham in an utter panic to find out if there really were poisonous snakes in France. He didn't know. There was an adder in Hardy, he said, who was never wrong about rural life, so possibly venomous snakes did live in temperate climes. He promised to look into it. He must have checked with Harold Nicolson because Nicolson called me the next day and tried to calm me down.

There were a few native vipers, he said, such as could kill a small dog, but nothing to worry about. 'Badgers kill them and eat them,' he said. 'Like mongoose in India.' He was one of those Englishmen who know everything, dead languages and modern art and politics in every country in the world and the way South Sea Islanders and hedgehogs mate. Not with each other, I mean, but what was usual in both sets. 'You didn't see the snake, did you?'

I said I hadn't. 'You don't think Bedaux keeps snakes? To discourage trespassers or reporters?'

'He's a bad sort, but I shouldn't think his methods would run to snakes. Too hard to keep track of. Not like having a tiger prowling the grounds. I'm sure it was an accident. He has no reason, I repeat, no reason in the world, to wish to harm you. You are the biggest card he's ever had to play. Watch him and you'll see.'

I decided then that I might as well be married at Candé. It was old and big and looked like Hollywood's idea of a castle. There was no hitch about my divorce, the decree became final in April, and the boy fled Enzesfeld and rushed to my side the minute the ink was dry. He couldn't wait to tie the knot. He wanted to get married right away and return by train to Austria, to the villa, Wasser-leonburg, that he rented in Carinthia. The itinerary was fine with me. We had to change trains at Venice, but I refused to be married before the Coronation. I wanted all that fuss to subside so the world could pay proper attention to me.

The coronation was set for May. It was broadcast around the world and the boy listened to it, sitting very still in a gilt chair in one of the château's ornate salons. I sat on another gilt chair for an hour or so, but it went on and on and I got bored. I couldn't bear to read about it either, but I did not generally read the newspapers, apart from the clippings that people continued to send me. Gossip columnists said that Hitler sent some old general, a *roué* whose taste in women was none too particular, possibly a not so delicate reminder that George VI owed it all to me, a *demi-mondaine*. The Ribbentrops gave a huge ball and invited all my old friends.[12] It would have been nice if they'd invited us, I'd have been tempted to go, but they didn't. The King of Italy was either not invited or refused to attend – the Coronation not the ball – because the Brits refused to give him the title of Emperor of Abyssinia, which seemed a little hypocritical because York and Cookie were being crowned Emperor and Empress of India. In fact, the only word I got first-hand about any of the celebrations came from my Indian friend. The maharajahs of all the little principalities came, and a handsome body of men they must have been. The darling sent me a postcard of Westminster Abbey, with a scrawl, 'Wish you were here! xxoo,' and his initial.

I fixed our wedding for June 3, as all the world knows, and I was run ragged arranging everything. My eager lover talked politics with Bedaux, who kept urging him to visit the New Germany, while I dealt with the florists and the caterers and the photographers and the little *maire* who was going to perform the civil ceremony and, at last, the only Protestant clergyman in England willing to travel to France to join us in holy matrimony.

Mainbocher worked for months, sending sketches of the dress and swatches of fabric for me to choose from. Coco Chanel, though really brilliant, was too modern and too smart to design my wedding dress. I wanted something more feminine and more traditional, in keeping with the medieval air of the château, and Mainbocher seemed the better choice. The dress could not be white, because it was not my first marriage, and it was his notion to call the colour, a flattering soft blue-grey, Windsor blue. I am and have always been grateful to him for his artistry.

Every detail had to be perfect – dress, hat, shoes, gloves, jewellery – because it looked like nobody would come except the press, and in the end almost no one did. The only word we got from the bridegroom's family was a flat refusal to let me be called Her Royal Highness.[13] The Rogerses brought Aunt Bessie, and Herman gave me away. The Duke's best man was Fruity Metcalfe, who'd been cuckolded by Oswald Mosley, so the British Union of Fascists was represented in an odd sort of way.[14] I must say that if my father was Lord Curzon, I'd have done better for myself than Fruity Metcalfe. Baron and Baroness Eugène de Rothschild sent an extremely lavish gift and showed up in person for the ceremony.[15] I was touched. Kitty said they spoke for many others who could not be present in wishing me happiness and, oddly, the Baron added, 'continued success.'

What does a woman remember about her honeymoon? This was my third and, as I suppose honeymoons are usually judged, not the best. Except for Venice. We stayed a day or two, more than we would have needed just to change trains, and an enormous lot of white carnations, a hundred at least, were delivered to our hotel. A gift from Mussolini,[16] who seemed to share Ribbentrop's taste in flowers. The Duke was beside himself that nothing came from Victor Emmanuel, King and Emperor, and he dawdled in our hotel, hoping for a word. At last, a naval officer arrived with another, smaller, box of flowers, beach roses, kept moist in seaweed. There was no note. 'Flown from Rhodes,' the man said, and very gallant and attractive he was. 'Where the Royal Visit will never be forgotten.'

Chapter Nine

Chapter Ten

The only good thing about Nazi Germany was that everybody called me 'Your Royal Highness' – everyone except Freddy von und zu Whatnot, who called me 'Your Grace,' which is what a Duchess is supposed to be called, and 'Ma'am' when we chatted, like the well-brought-up boy he was. He was ordered back to Berlin to squire me around and possibly also to annoy Ribbentrop, who was not there when we first arrived. No one seemed to like him in Germany either.

Charles Bedaux made all the arrangements for our trip and he was very pushy about making sure we went. Not that my husband needed much pushing. He was keen to go because he'd heard so much about all the Nazis had done for the workers.

Bedaux visited us several times during our honeymoon at Wasserleonburg, smaller than Schloss Enzesfeld but nothing to sneeze at either, and it was a hoot to hear the two of them, surrounded by antlers and tapestries and paintings, in rooms cluttered with silver and porcelain, going on and on about the poor. Workers' housing, it turned out, was supposed to be the purpose of our trip to Germany. The Duke would be invited as a private person to look at various charitable projects, because of his profound knowledge and deep concern for the welfare of the poor. Bedaux made a point of this: we would meet philanthropists, he said, and visionaries, and no party hacks or petty officials.[1] It might be necessary before leaving to pay a visit to Hitler at Berchtesgaden, but that would be private too, nothing official, just one country gentleman visiting another's country seat. The man fancied himself a country gentleman because he bought his château rather than renting it, and you would have thought his family had lived there since the dawn of time.

We arrived in Berlin in October, and it turned out, no surprise, to be red carpets and brass bands and goose-stepping flunkies from the moment we arrived. We were met by a Nazi official, Robert Ley, who had some connection with their labour movement, lots of uniformed men, and a pathetic handful of very junior Brits. The ambassador, Sir Nevile Henderson, had been suddenly called away, something that would often happen when we turned up in a European capital. There were no philanthropists or industrialists, or none I ever saw.[2]

I had worried about what to wear. Bedaux, though he pretended to be a French aristocrat, advised me not to look 'too French.' I had my maid pack mostly black, which could be easily accessorised for the local colour scheme. I bought a new ermine cape and packed all my rubies. For the weekend we were supposed to spend at Berchtesgaden, 'in the country', I brought a shapeless tweed coat and a plain felt hat.

On our first evening in Berlin, we had an informal supper with several Nazis, I forget which ones. They did not all look alike. They all looked odd in different ways, except Rudolf Hess, who was not bad-looking. I have to say, the Nazis did not beat around the bush. They put it to the Duke that they were going to conquer England and restore him as King with myself as his Queen. They talked a lot to him about how deeply he must feel his family's insults to his wife. 'No matter, she vill be Her Majesty soon enough. And you vill haff no more troubles about the Royal Highness-ing.'

The men who spoke English called it 'the Restoration'. At first Boysy was not sure this was a good idea, but it didn't take them long to convince him.

'You'll be careful,' he said. 'Not to hurt anyone, civilians, for example. I wouldn't want violence of any kind, no bloodshed, none of that sort of thing.'

They expected to be met by cheering crowds, they said, if England's true King, loved by all, and his pure and noble wife, also loved by all, came with them. 'That is why your co-operation is essential,' one of them said. 'When we are coming Your Royal Highnesses to restore, our victory will not be needing blood to shed.'

'Virtually bloodless,' another explained.

I don't know anything about politics, but, as I may have mentioned, I know when men are lying.

My husband said he'd think it over. He'd come to their splendid country as a private person, not to discuss matters of state. Later that night he told me he didn't like to decline. It's rude to refuse a gift that one's host is pressing upon one.

We spent most of our time with Ley, who drank from early morning. He took us to some other cities, Munich and Nuremberg, but we were in Berlin most of the time, and in the capital there were all sorts of things I wasn't invited to – stag dinners and lunches and meetings and one long afternoon with their Navy people that Boysy got a little huffy when asked about. 'Need-to-know basis, my darling. No need to trouble your beautiful head.' That worried me. I would not have that fool telling me what should and should not trouble my head. The sooner I got him out of Germany, the better.

One evening, after a day of stag events, he positively glowed. 'They were right at Oxford, my angel bunny. I'm not the sort of man who needs books to learn about things. I have a higher order of intelligence. I grasp things as they really are. They have a word for it in German.'

'For your kind of intelligence?'

'No, you precious little silly, for the thing I can grasp.'

'How nice,' I said.

'Some people attach too much importance to books, and I used to feel bad that I couldn't see the point of them. I see now how wrong I was when really I was right all along. They burn books here every now and then. Very sound.'

During the serious business, Freddy took me to parks and museums. He thought I'd be interested in the Egyptian things, of which there were a lot. 'We used to be great Orientalists,' he said, standing in front of the bust of a woman. 'Isn't she wonderful?'

'Is that what Cleopatra really looked like?'

'Possibly, but it's much earlier. Eighteenth Dynasty or there-abouts. I hope she'll be safe.'

'Why shouldn't she be safe? She's in a glass case in a museum.'

'Oh, never mind. Mustn't have any defeatist talk,' he said, and I wasn't sure what he meant.

The jewellery in that museum was too gorgeous for words, brilliant enamel and gold in fantastic shapes, birds and snakes and those scarab beetles that were becoming so fashionable. It would be perfect for summer, with just the sort of simple white linen and cotton I'd worn in Egypt. I asked if I could have some and Freddy said he'd see what he could do.

At the end of the first week, Göring and his wife, the couple the Lindberghs knew, gave us a formal dinner followed by dancing. Hitler we were yet to see, and Freddy told me that he was a vegetarian and a teetotaller and did not dance, did not like High Society, *Feinen Leute*, so between them the Göbbelses and the Görings got to do most of the entertaining of foreign guests. Frau Göring was exactly what Anne Lindbergh described, in red velvet this time with a large diamond, ruby, and black enamel swastika. I was wearing more and better rubies[3] with a new and very good black satin dress.

All the most important people, party and army, were there and, finally, they wanted to talk to me, about my life in the American South. They seemed to take their racial theories very seriously. Lightning Brain told them he saw Aborigines during his tour of Australia as Prince of Wales. 'They looked like monkeys,'[4] he recalled. 'I do not believe to this day they are actually human. My aides silenced me at the time. I was never permitted to speak my mind, to tell the truth as I saw it.' Germany was doing wonders for his self-confidence.

'We vill see to that. You vill soon haff no Kappinett to trouble you.' Some of them spoke English well and some sounded like a comedy routine.

They talked about the mongrelisation of France, that Frenchmen were all pimps or fops who could never fight another war because they were exhausted by debauchery. Constant debauchery. Orgies day and night that never stopped. They were surprised we planned to make our home among such a depraved people. The Nazis seemed very troubled by the sex other people were having and they were not.

Then they talked about how disappointed they were with Mussolini. He and Count Ciano had been there a few weeks before. I wished I'd known, because honeymooning didn't keep me terribly busy and we could have made the trip earlier. Apparently Mussolini was dallying over some racial laws they wanted him to enact. They described the provisions of these laws for mating, who could and could not do the deed together, in revolting detail. Faced with that freak show of Supermen, I would have violated their sex laws at the first opportunity.

'The Italians couple shamelessly,' one of them said. 'They have no conception of purity. Mussolini's had a Jewish mistress, as all the world knows, for years,[5] a few others known to us, and who knows how many more?'

'His daughter has a Jewish lover,'[6] another said. 'And Ciano is so depraved himself that he permits it.' Maybe Gallo didn't care what she did. That was a cheering thought, but whether he cared or didn't care, he'd certainly never need to pass a law to get women to go to bed with him.

'Mussolini does not have enough mimeograph machines to distribute the text,' somebody said with a laugh, one of the few men present that evening who could not have been part of a carnival sideshow.[7] 'He'll get around to it. Mustn't be too hard on them.'

Then another man, very strange-looking, spoke more seriously. 'The Italians lack the will and they lack the tools. We should depend on them for nothing.'

I am afraid a sigh escaped me. Then this very odd man – Freddy later told me his name was Himmler – asked me if I had ever been insulted by a Negro. He seemed to hope that I had and that I would tell him about it.

I hadn't been insulted, certainly not, most charmingly entertained. I thought I'd better not tell them about my African adventures. 'We were too poor to have darkies. My more fortunate friends tell me their servants are very loyal.'

Freddy tried to explain the difference between house slaves and field slaves, but no one listened to him.

'Your lands ver stolen. Ach, vat a catastrophe. Ve understand catastrophe. Alzo ve suffert haff. Didj'yew know' – this was Göring, addressing the table at large –'that the Jew Abraham Lin–Cohen slaughtered all the vite planterz? Shot them dead efen after they offert up their swords and divided their lantz among the blacks? Effery one of those savages got forty acres and a mule.'

'Confederate officers were amnestied,' Freddy said. 'Their lands weren't confiscated, not that some people weren't proposing it.'

'Zo.' Göring had finally heard something Freddy said. 'Can you explain, then, Herr Graf von und zu something or other, how it vass that twenty years after the var all the vealth of the South vass in the hanz of Jew Yankee plutocrats?'

Freddy said he could not.

'Ve vill avenge you, Your Royal Highness,' Göring promised. 'Ve vill obliterate all your enemies, past, present, and future.' It did not bode well for Cookie, their invasion. 'But, come, let us tanze.'

I am not sure what the 'bloated Alcibiades' attempted with poor little Anne Lindbergh, but with me he was the classic groper, pincher, and fanny-slapper. Worse than many, because his fingers seemed made for clawing and scraping.[8] He may have grasped ideas as quickly as my husband. He certainly grabbed me, and it hurt.

He insisted on a second waltz and danced me out onto the terrace of his house, where it was very dark. 'You haff your KKK, Your Royal Highness. Do you know about ours?'

'No, but do tell me all about it, and could we go inside? It's chilly out here.' That was a mistake. He took off his coat and wrapped it around me so tightly I could not move my arms.

'For our vomen,' he said, 'it is alzo KKK: *Kirke, Kinder, Küche*. Church, Children, and Kitchen.'

'How nice for them,' I said.

'Ach, Your Royal Highness, ve haff another K, '*der Küss*' – kissing and all that follows kissing.' He grabbed me and tried to force his beery tongue between my teeth. Where was my adorable Nubian, I wondered, when I really needed him – him, his spear, and every single one of his red ants? Göring's flesh would feed all the ants in Africa, red and black, for years to come.

It was Freddy who came to my rescue in a European way. 'Oh, hello, there you are.' He was looking for me for the next dance. 'Forgive the interruption, Herr General, the lady has promised me the polka.'

'Her Royal Highness has promised you the polka,' Göring thundered.

'Right-oh, HRH it is.' He helped me out of Göring's heavy uniform coat and took my hand to lead me back inside. The young *graf* had a way of taking charge.

'Gut. Go and tanze, the two of you,' Göring said. 'Ve must all learn Polish tanzes.'

I was thankful after that evening that we were going to Berchtesgaden for the weekend. I arrived looking like a charwoman in the tweed coat and felt hat, and I must say, I did not lower the tone of the place. Hitler's mistress. Eva Braun, appeared in peasant costume. She did not even try for county dowdy. She wore puffed sleeves, a tight bodice with silver buttons, and a dirndl skirt, and because she also wore a lot of make-up not applied with much skill, she looked like something out of the chorus of an operetta performed by a touring company very much down on its luck.

Some people said that Hitler had a strange magnetism, that he was hypnotic. He struck me as having no charm and no manners. He bit his fingernails and he was always patting his moustache, as if it was glued on and he was afraid it might fall off. I do not speak German, so I could not understand anything he said to Lightning Brain or that LB said to him during their long and chummy talks. Boysy was fluent in German and talked more cheerfully with Hitler than I'd ever seen him do with an English politician. Most of the time, if women were allowed in the room with the Great Men, Eva Braun knitted and I sat primly with my hands in my lap, thinking of the clothes I would order when I got back to France. The only thing Hitler said to me during the entire weekend was 'Your Royal Highness,' which he said each time he looked at me, which was not often, generally at the beginning and end of meals. He may have been a vegetarian, but he did not appear to believe in green salads.

This weekend in Berchtesgaden was supposed to be absolutely private. Bedaux had said that over and over, but there were plenty of photographers around all the time, inside the house as well as in the grounds. I didn't think much about it, except for what a frump I looked, so imagine my surprise when the picture was printed, me in that hat and coat that looked like cook's night out, with Hitler proclaiming to the world that I would make a 'wonderful Queen'. Ribbentrop made a point of announcing in London the Führer's grief and outrage that 'a clique of reactionaries and Marxists' had prevented the King of England from marrying 'a girl of the people'.[9] The British embassy, which was taking no official notice of our presence in Germany, sent a bushel of newspapers to our hotel so I would not miss a word. Someone was kind enough to explain in a note that came with the papers that, though reactionaries and Marxists might not always see eye to eye, the phrase evoked a Nazi song, the 'Horst Wessel Lied', which spoke of *die Rotfront* (the

Reds) *und Reaktion*, so the words would strike a familiar chord. The meaning would be widely understood and long remembered. The wretched little vulgar worm. I was ready for the war that people said was coming.

People said one of Hitler's balls had been shot off in the war, and other people said it had been bitten off by a goat during his unhappy childhood, possibly by the outraged father or brother of the nanny goat he was attempting to mount. I was ready to cut off the other one. Of all the terrible things I had been called in the past, no one, not Queen Mary, not Cookie, not the cheapest tabloid, had ever suggested that I belonged to 'the people'.

I was happy to return to Berlin, even if it did mean Göring and, as it turned out, Ribbentrop also. He returned with his champagne heiress wife to give a dinner for us at their ostentatious new house, Sonnenburg, on the outskirts of Berlin. I didn't want to go at first, after what he'd said about me. Then I decided I would go and wear the tiara I'd brought with me in case an occasion arose, and really let him have it. I wore black satin and ermine – it was a floor-length cape, not one of those little ones that just go round your shoulders – and enough diamonds and rubies to build a substantial house for every worker in Germany and the British Isles.

Ribbentrop said I looked like a Queen and I said, didn't he mean a goose girl? He kissed both my hands and explained that ladies, even Queens, did not understand propaganda. I was too refined to imagine what common folk wanted to hear. If he told them how divine I was, I might lose their sympathy and support. I should leave everything to him and all would be well. He would weep with joy when he saw me crowned in Westminster, looking as regal as I looked tonight, bringing the splendour of an Empire to his humble abode.

He kept near me all evening, very chatty and confidential, showing me his paintings, of which he was very proud. We gossiped about the Coronation and he told me how furious it made him, the injustice of it all and how much I had suffered. 'I am preparing a lengthy report on British politics for the Führer. I have concluded that His Gracious Majesty Edward VIII was forced from his throne because of his outspoken friendship for the German people and his admiration for our Leader.'[10]

'You are a very clever man,' I said, and I gave him my hands to kiss again for everyone to see. Anyone watching us would have thought we were, at the very least, good friends. It was not my worst day in Germany.

The worst day was the next, which was, thank God, also the last. There was an endless luncheon at the Air Club. Anne Lindbergh told me Göring liked to entertain foreigners there because he was very proud of the interior decoration, which he did himself.[11] Nothing about it appealed to me. The meal was like every meal in Germany, only more so. There were more kinds of sausages than I thought there could be in the world and lots of roast birds and animals, and no vegetables but potatoes. I sat next to Göring, and at that point I did want to talk to him because people said he was influential, and I wanted him to know I came from a good family. It was stupid, I know, but that 'people' business upset me. It was so unfair.

'Everyone says your Leader respects you,' I began, trying to flatter him. 'I wish you'd tell him he's misinformed about my background.'

'The Führer is neffer misinformed,' he corrected me. 'His knowledge of a subject can, howeffer, be deepened.'

'I wish you'd deepen it, then. I come from an old and very distinguished family. I had my family tree done.' I'd looked into this some years ago, after collecting all the documents I needed about my divorce, to get presented at Court. I was foolish enough then to think some good ancestors might help me with the Royals.

'Eggszellent,' he said. 'You can not be too careful.'

'I was poor, before my marriage, and these family trees cost the

Chapter Ten

earth. They wanted $250 and I refused to pay that much for some dusty old records. I simply could not afford it, and in the end I got it for $150.'[12]

'Zo, Your Royal Highness, you "jewed" them down.' He seemed to think this very funny and he had a very unattractive laugh. He slid his hand beneath the tablecloth and squeezed my leg. 'You say that in England, Your Royal Highness, "jew them down"?'

'Some people do,' I said, trying to dislodge his hand. 'Oh, my goodness, I've dropped my napkin. Can you get it for me?'

He motioned for a waiter with his other hand and tightened his grip. 'The English do not lack knowledge of danger,' he said. 'They lack the vill and the courage to fight it. Ve Germans hold fast.'

Dessert was served. A variety of cakes and some fruit, all stewed together and unrecognisable as any particular kind.

'Ve vill go tonight to the opera,' he said when the coffee came and I thought I was nearly done with him. 'I hear you like opera.'

'Thank you, but my husband doesn't care for it at all.'

'Zo? Himmler will take him to vatch our beautiful youth doing their gymnastic egg-zercises. They vill haff a good time and ve,' he leered, 'vill haff an even better time.' He continued to grope and clutch as he had throughout the meal, but now he was more insistent, breathing down my neck and nibbling my ear. 'German operas last twice as long as the Italians'. Ve haff stamina.' He bit my ear, hard. 'I know you like it. *Aida.*' He snorted. 'How sweet, how gallant. "In his thoughts you are a Queen". Your little *contino* cannot make you a Queen, Duchess.' Gallo was not little. He was just right, and Göring was a fat pig. 'I, and only I, can do that.'

'I cannot go to the opera with you tonight, sir,' I said. 'I have a headache.'

The Nazis really did make my head ache, and I didn't want to be Queen of England with Göring pawing my thigh.

Chapter Eleven

Paris was grey and the trees were bare and if orgies were going on, we weren't invited. It never looked better to me than it did after Berlin. It was a relief to be back in our own little *pied-à-terre* in the Hôtel Meurice. Everyone knew where we'd been. The concierge was cool on our return, and most of the staff were chilly too, polite but not cordial. My masseuse, on the other hand, saw all my scratches and bruises. She sympathised with me and she was furious with my husband: How could *M'sieur le duc* take such a lady to such a place? Had he not fought the *Boches* the last time? Did he not know that a man's first duty is to protect his wife? She had higher expectations of him than I had.

We were living in a hotel because we hadn't yet found a house of our own. Boysy wanted to live in the country, I wanted to live in the city, and I hadn't been able to convince him that the Bois de Boulogne was rural. It took me almost another year to do that. That winter he set his mind, such as it was, against spending Christmas in a hotel, or, for that matter, in Paris, period, or full stop, as he said. He'd picked up the idea somewhere that the French, or the people in charge in France, were godless atheists as well as sex fiends. I gathered that he heard nothing good about gay Paree during all those stag events in Germany, and as Ribbentrop told Emerald Cunard, the Führer was keeping his options open on religious matters.

Very well, I said, let's leave the wicked French and go to Rome. There's plenty of religion there. He'd enjoyed the Nazis. He might like the Fascists too, if he got to know them. He would not hear of it. Unthinkable to visit a monarchy except at the invitation of its Sovereign, and he was still sulking over Victor Emmanuel's failure

Chapter Eleven

to welcome us to Rhodes or to Venice. I thought winter in Rome might be nice, not too cold, and they had a King and a Court, so I imagined there would be balls. I'd never danced with Gallo and I would have liked to. It's hard, though, to dance with a man and hide your feelings for him. You can pretend to like him more than you do. I'd done that with Boysy in London nightclubs for years, but the reverse is harder. I'd been able to do it in Washington, years ago, but I wasn't sure I could do it now, with him.

With Rome out and Spain at war, our choices were limited, and there were places we could not go – England, for example, or the United States. Boysy didn't seem to grasp how much damage our German jaunt had done us. We were planning to tour the United States in the spring to look more deeply into the New Deal. It was only fair, he said, to see how Roosevelt's projects compared with Hitler's brilliant success, everything so clean and orderly and people working like beavers, and I wanted to show my native land how marvellous I looked despite all I suffered from the snobbery and prejudice of Certain Persons.

Sad to say, it was made plain to us almost immediately after we returned to France that we would not be welcome in America. The Duke had a ranch in Alberta, but we couldn't go to Canada either, or any of the Dominions, until things got settled about how we could ever go back to England. They were threatening to cut off our allowance if the Duke set foot in Britain without the approval of the King 'under the advice of his ministers'. I helped him write a long, firm letter to the Prime Minister. Baldwin, who'd been so difficult at the time of the Abdication, had retired and the new one, Neville Chamberlain, was no improvement. I made our letter proud and bitter: this requirement was 'unfair and intolerable, as it would be tantamount to my accepting payment for remaining in exile'.[1] Chamberlain never replied, so we accepted payment to remain in exile and continued to sponge off our friends to save money.

We spent Christmas 1937 in Cannes with Herman and Katherine

Rogers. We didn't go to the Casino or to church on Christmas Eve, we stayed up till midnight so I could open my present. I couldn't wait until Christmas morning to see what I'd get this year, now that I was a married lady not a kept woman. I almost fainted dead away when I opened the box and found a Cartier panther, legs extended, leaping after his prey, emerald eyes and diamond body with black onyx spots, not square-cut but round like the rosettes that mark the East African leopard.[2] I felt sure Coco Chanel was responsible. There were so few women I could confide in and I'd told Coco almost everything. Coco had been the Duke of Westminster's mistress for years and she got on well with Englishmen. My husband knew how close we were and he often asked her advice about what to buy for me. This time her intuition and the attention to detail, for which she is so justly famous, took my breath away.

War was raging in Asia that winter. I guess that Chiang Kai-shek did not take the deal, if one was offered to him, of co-operating with the Japanese and fighting the Communists instead. People said that his wife's sister was close to the Reds, so possibly those girls, unlike the Mitfords, made up their differences when their country was in danger. Things were tense in Europe too, though there was no shooting except in Spain. Then, in the spring of 1938, the Germans marched into Austria. This was something a lot of people expected, apparently, and even my husband knew was coming: he'd seen a map in Göring's library that had Austria, where we'd spent our honeymoon, printed blue, the same as Germany. I guess it must have been the same one that Anne Lindbergh saw, but Lightning Brain wasn't concerned about France or Poland. When he'd asked Göring about it, he said it would happen soon and 'voluntarily.' In fairness to the Duke, when it actually did happen, he said Göring had a funny idea of 'voluntarily'.[3] That ghastly man had a lot of funny ideas.

Eugène and Kitty Rothschild, the Baroness with not a hair out of place, got safely to France with stories of how bad it had been. Very bad, she said. People they knew had been beaten up and arrested and actually killed. Many had simply disappeared and many others had committed suicide. She spoke about it calmly, cold and grim. Nothing rattled Kitty, not even the Nazis.

I invited her to come with me to see the couture collection for the next season, to take her mind off her troubles. The clothes they were showing were spectacular – gorgeous fabrics, silk taffetas, everything glistening and rustling, nothing matte, lots of glass beads and *paillettes*, cascades of lace and gold-embroidered bolero jackets – fantastically lavish.[4] I, for one, was determined to buy them, wear them, and look like an Empress and not let the world get me down. We went to the Ritz after the show. Neither of us felt like tea and I ordered a bottle of champagne.

'Those clothes,' Kitty said. '*Après moi le déluge.*' I knew what she meant. People said that all the time in those days. 'I wish the storm would break. It enrages me that people are letting the Nazis run away with the world.'

I asked her how they escaped. 'We paid,' she said. 'And we had to spend considerably more and sign away major assets, including factories in Czechoslovakia, to ransom my brother-in-law, who stayed longer than was really wise. I will say, though, the Austrians can be bought. Their venality is their most charming quality.'

The looting, she said, was beyond belief. They and most collectors had been sending paintings out of the country for years, on extended loan to American museums or to Switzerland for cleaning. 'One expects soldiers will pillage,' she said. 'But not Cabinet Ministers. Would you believe your old beau Ribbentrop walked off with Metternich's globe?'[5]

'He's capable of anything,' I said, but I could not see why this disturbed her as much as it obviously did.

'Göring was the worst, as you'd expect. He stole a Stradivarius that Eugène's father gave to a musical friend. But the loss I feel the most deeply . . . ' She must have felt it deeply, because she was tough and it took her a few minutes to find the words to tell me about it. She sipped her champagne. 'Did you know that barbarian fancies himself a Renaissance man? Though,' she said with a smile, 'I expect he doesn't meet your high standards.'

'I don't like him at all. He claims to like opera. What's his pleasure in art? Naked ladies?'

'If only he'd confined himself to the flabby nudes, Austria could spare him plenty of those. You know that glorious, golden, almost Byzantine Klimt portrait of the woman wearing a diamond choker?'

'Who doesn't?' I for one.

'Göring took the painting *and the necklace*.[6] Adele died years ago, of meningitis, poor darling,' Kitty said. 'She'd left her jewels to her sister and Göring got the lot.'

'A diamond choker? Quite high?'

'Very. Adele was an exquisite creature with a neck like a swan.'

'It should be some consolation then,' I said, remembering the couple, 'to know that Göring's wife is not quite a cow but she is no swan. A diamond choker will fit her like a neck brace. It will do nothing for her.'

'Thank you, Wallis,' Kitty said. 'You are a comfort.'

'All those marvellous clothes we saw today should cheer you up. You should get some, Kitty. Elegance is a comfort.'

'Speaking of elegance, why didn't you tell me that Margherita Sarfatti was going to Argentina?'

'Who's Margherita Sarfatti?'

I didn't know it was possible for anyone, even the Baroness Rothschild, to raise her eyebrows that high. 'Really, Wallis.' She was going to say more, but she stopped herself. She had tremendous self-control.

'I don't know what you're talking about. I've never heard of her.'

Kitty took a cheese straw and bit into it. She finished it and gestured to the waiter, who refilled our glasses. She took a sip of champagne and then another. 'Very well. I'll tell you because it might interest you. Margherita Sarfatti and Mussolini have been lovers, on and off, and mostly on, for twenty years. She scooped him up into her brilliant Futurist salon and introduced him to everyone who was anyone in Milan when he was just another randy young socialist nobody.'

'She's the Jewish mistress?' And elegant and brilliant and Futurist? She must be old, though. 'I didn't know her name.'

'Whatever you say. She's never criticised him publicly.[7] I don't know if she, or anyone else, ever criticises him in private. And,' she said, pausing to take another cheese straw, 'I'm not asking if you know.'

'I'm not interested in politics.'

'Indeed. Suffice to say Signora Sarfatti is keenly interested in politics. She took up with him because he was a radical who named his first child after a character in Ibsen.'

'Edda?'

'Hedda Gabler. Names don't start with an *H* in Italian.' Kitty knew things like that. 'He is no longer advanced, sad to say, or he's advancing in another direction. The canary in the coal mine has flown the coop. It can't be a good sign.'

More and more refugees poured into Paris from all over Europe, and France and England waited, holding their breath and getting chummier by the minute. A Royal Visit to Paris was planned for the summer of 1938. We were told to get out of town in order to avoid any awkwardness that might arise when we met or did not meet the King and Queen, and that presented an opportunity to rent a place of our own, La Croë at Cap d'Antibes.

Cookie made a tremendous hit with the French. Her mother died right before they were supposed to arrive and the trip could not be postponed because of the international situation, and that posed a problem because she could not wear black all the time in Paris in the summer. English couture, or, as Coco said, English dressmaking, scored an amazing coup. Cookie wowed everyone with an entirely white wardrobe.[8] White counts as mourning for summer clothes, and she looked, well . . . I thought she looked like a

virginal wet nurse, with those womanly bosoms of hers. But everyone else said she looked like a true lady and womanly woman and a
Queen who would give away her last crumb of cake to the poor and
a Grande Dame and a Great Beauty and a vision from the happy
days before the Great War. She was praised to the skies. *Le tout
Paris*, the most blasé and cynical, went wild over her, and the rest of
France worshipped her. She spoke French all the time, of course,
the way those girls do who did everything they were supposed to do
when they were young. When I happened to see her quoted, I
couldn't understand most of what she said. She seemed to have
memorised the endings for every verb. Other women dressed well at
the parties they gave for her. For the reception at the Élysée Palace,
Daisy Fellowes, our neighbour on the Riviera, wore a gorgeous dress,
a white silk *marquisine* Schiaparelli [9] embroidered with silver flowers.
Daisy was an old girlfriend of Duff's, very rich, and, next to me,
probably the best-dressed woman in the world, but people barely
glanced at her, she told me – they were mesmerised by the Queen.

I was glad I wasn't in Paris while Cookie was there, and I was very
happy about being settled in a house of my own on the Riviera. We
made a comfortable home with our little household, my maid who'd
been with me through thick and thin, and men who had been with
the Duke since Enzesfeld – his private secretary, Percival Dreggs,
and Major Grey Philips of the Black Watch. The major was a
confirmed bachelor and we got on very well. He was not too military
or too proud to help me with little chores like planning menus or
arranging flowers. Most of the house servants and the cook were
French. She came to us from a wealthy and titled French family,
and she was very good. The gardeners were mixed, French and
Italian. Our house was not far from the border, and I was quick to
seize that opportunity too.

Gallo was born in Tuscany [10] and he was devoted to his father,
the old admiral Costanzo Ciano, who still lived there. He came
north often and I managed to get word to him to arrange a meeting.

Nice and Genoa are much closer than Washington and New York, and between them there are lots of places perfect for romantic meetings, much better than the Atlantic coast.

We met first in San Remo. The hotel Gallo chose for our rendez-vous was small and discreet, with a terrace that could be entered from the street. I walked up some palm-shaded steps and there he was, sitting at a table beneath a big flowering bush. He never smoked, and he was reading a book to pass the time, with a little coffee cup and a pot of espresso on the table before him. Whatever he was reading seemed to engross him, and he didn't look up until I stood between him and the sun. 'Hello,' I said, and he sprang to his feet and took me into his arms and, without another word, took me upstairs. Hours later he asked if I was hungry. I was, ravenous. 'Your poor famished body,' he said, kissing me everywhere. 'Can't the English even feed you?' We hadn't seen each other for two years and somehow, once we were together, it seemed we'd never been apart.

We had a weekend in Portofino. I was supposed to be in Monte-catini at a spa with Katherine Rogers, and Herman was keeping Boysy occupied. The Rogerses could not have been more helpful or understanding. Daisy Fellowes too, whose villa at Cap Martin was practically in Italy, was very kind and told me to treat her house as my own. There were limits, though, to what sympathetic friends could do. That weekend was the only time Gallo and I ever spent the night together. On Sunday morning he took me to a rocky promontory where, he said, the colours of the sea were unequalled anywhere in the world. He was very serious about it and I teased him. 'Says who?'

'The Touring Club of Milan,'[11] he said. 'It's in the *Guide Bleu*.' When we got back to the villa where we were staying, he showed me the page. 'It should have more stars,' he said, marking three in the margin, and he gave me the book so that I could read about all the beautiful places we would go together. He loved that coast and I think he felt it belonged to him, and in a way I suppose it did. I loved Portofino, and being there with him was Heaven on earth. Fashionable resorts, however, offer very little privacy. Big cities are more anonymous, so we met mostly in Genoa.

It wasn't easy. Tensions were increasing then, not just between England and France and Germany, but also between Italy and France. I am sorry to say that Gallo himself was partly to blame, because he kept insisting that Nice and Corsica should be returned to Italy. Tunisia too. I couldn't imagine why anyone would want Tunisia, but he said it had to do with Rome and Carthage and the French had no historic claim to it. There was talk too, as there always seemed to be, about the Suez Canal. I wouldn't have minded if Italy got Nice, or Cannes and Antibes, for that matter. It didn't seem such a bad idea to me. There were a number of beautiful villas, like Daisy's place, that would make a perfect summer residence for the Foreign Minister. Gallo said I was as amusing as I was beautiful.

We didn't see each other often. Quite apart from politics, it's more difficult than I ever imagined to have an affair with a man who isn't part of your set: You can't go to the country for the weekend and steal an afternoon while the others are golfing or shooting or dead-heading roses or watching pheasants hatch, and then spend half the night together. You can't have lunch or tea at a smart hotel where you go all the time and people are used to seeing you and nobody notices if you leave the table and slip upstairs. Sometimes the powder room is on the mezzanine and you can actually get into an elevator. Being married to a man who wants to be with you every minute of every day makes it harder, naturally, but what made it, in the end, impossible was that everyone in the world knew what I looked like. There are disadvantages to being Woman of the Year. Gallo wasn't as famous as I was, but he was a public figure with duties he took seriously and children, three of them, he insisted on seeing in much of his free time.

His responsibilities did worry him sometimes. One afternoon he wasn't his usual sunny self and I asked what was wrong.

'Napoleon,' he said. 'I was thinking about Corsica and naturally I thought of him.'

'So why does that make you glum, apart from that France has it at the moment?' Politics did not really interest me then.

He said he was thinking of something else entirely. 'He invaded Russia.'

'Yes,' I said, 'I know, and it ended badly, but that was after he left the beautiful *divorcée* who was the love of his life and married an Austrian cow.' My manicurist liked to talk about Napoleon and I thought it served him right.

'Exactly. *After* he made sure of Austria. It is a bad mistake to invade Russia. Your friend Duff Cooper wrote an excellent book . . .'[12] And he went on to talk about a man who tried to do what was best for France after a catastrophic defeat. He said Duff saw things very clearly. I should tell Duff they thought alike about many things but that Il Duce hadn't liked the book at all.

'Please, Gallo,' I said, 'let's not talk any more. I can't stay much longer.'

'You are right,' he said. 'Deeds not words. Much better.'

The hours we had were wonderful. I can't begin to say how wonderful. I couldn't put it into words. But it couldn't last. People recognised me and, I was pretty sure, sometimes followed me, and the next time I came to Genoa, Gallo told me we had to stop seeing each other. There was too much at stake, and if we were found out, it would be far worse for me than for him. In Italy, he said, people understood things that possibly in England they did not understand so well, and everywhere, the world judges women more harshly than it judges men. 'You can't escape reporters and photographers, and British intelligence must be watching you, and the Germans.'

'Göring knew about Rhodes. He even knew what opera we saw.' Gallo said it didn't surprise him. 'Are there spies in Genoa?' I asked.

'Are there worms in cheese? It's too dangerous. Today must be the last time.'

I am afraid that I started to cry, not because I thought my tears could change his mind – he wasn't that sort of man – but because I was so unhappy. I remember what I wore that day, a tussah silk short-sleeved summer suit in the Windsor blue of my wedding dress, which is very becoming, and the chalcedony and sapphire bracelets and ear clips I'd worn the last evening in Rhodes. I didn't think as I put them on in the morning that this would be another farewell.

'*Poverina,* poor little thing.' I was weeping like a child and he took me onto his lap. 'I am sad for you.' I simply could not stop crying. 'I am sad for you,' he repeated. 'Truly. You deserve better.' He held me closer. 'Your husband is impotent,[13] isn't he?'

'How do you know?' I was so startled that my tears stopped. 'Did your spies find that out? Do other countries know?'

'You're the Mata Hari. You have told me yourself, in many ways.'

'I have, haven't I?' It was mortifying to be so desperate.

'It is obvious, when one thinks about it. Keeping mistresses does not prevent kings from marrying, even in England. Why is it that no Royal Family in Europe and no British peer would give a daughter to this man, the richest and greatest King in the world? It must be because a modern girl, even a good and obedient girl, would refuse to marry without sex. A family would fear, if they forced her, she might disgrace herself, and them, afterwards.'

I began to cry again, more quietly this time. I felt very sorry for myself. Gallo could not have been more different from my husband, not just because of his manliness but because he understood things. 'When can I see you again?'

'In the *dopoguerra.*'

'What's that?'

'After the war. I forget you don't know modern idioms. The war is coming, but it won't last forever.'

'Will you fight?'

'If I have to. We may be neutral this time. Non-belligerents.'

Chapter Eleven

'If you got Nice, would you still have to fight? Is Corsica really necessary?' I'd gotten rid of a King – how hard could it be to get a city? I wasn't sure who the Premier of France was at the moment, but it didn't matter, I was sure I could manage it. If German pressure would help, I'd sleep with Göring. There was nothing, nothing in the world, I wouldn't have done to get Gallo what he wanted and keep him safe, and I explained my plan.

'Göring!' he almost shouted. 'The last time I saw him, he was wearing a ruby pinned to his tie, rubies on his fingers, and a diamond Nazi eagle in his buttonhole. He looked like Al Capone.[14] You must never let Göring make love to you, Wallis, or Ribbentrop. Never, not for any reason. Promise me.'

I promised.

We'd spent the afternoon in an apartment that belonged to one of his high school classmates. A closed car was idling in the alley behind the building, and Gallo drove with me to the old port, where his friend was waiting with a fast boat to take me to San Remo. He handed me into the boat and said, '*Addio, adieu,*' which means this really is the end. He nodded to his friend and in seconds, it seemed, we sped off into the Bay of Genoa.

His friend looked like he'd be a cheery fellow at happier moments, but he saw the state I was in and he treated me with the awful respect women get in some parts of the world when they belong to powerful men. I'd seen it before, but never in England, where nobody was afraid of Lightning Brain. He was silent most of the way, handling the boat alone and using binoculars to scan the sea and sky for other boats or low-flying planes. Once or twice he waved to a sailboat. 'No worries,' he said. 'We are in Italian waters and I have a radio.'

As we approached the coast, he spoke again. 'Things will get better, *signora, madama,* but first they will get worse.' Not an original thought in 1938, but I felt he meant it kindly.

An older man, small, wiry, and deeply suntanned, was waiting for us at the pier with a car, not large and not new and rather dusty. He apologised for the car. 'This automobile is not fit for a great lady,' he said. 'But there is a reason. If we are stopped, I am to say that your automobile broke down and I am taking you to the house of your friend.' He drove me quickly away from the harbour and up into the hills on back roads, a roundabout way to Daisy Fellowes's place where I'd supposedly spent the day. He said little else, except that he liked the English. They were good sailors. I thought he might have been a man loyal to Gallo's father, maybe an old shipmate. When he left me at Daisy's, he said, '*Addio, principessa. Good luck.' Principessa* – a royal title was the least of what I would never have as Boysy's wife. No one would honour me or protect me out of respect for him. I'd have to take care of myself. But I was used to that.

Chapter Eleven

Chapter Twelve

Ambassador Kennedy's job required his wife to dine with the 'tart' on at least one occasion, in Paris in February of 1939.[1] Maybe at that point he regarded me as a reformed tart, like some prominent saints, or maybe diplomatic service made him lax. The American ambassador to France invited us to a party he was giving for the American ambassador to Poland and other US diplomats in Europe. I guess they were all getting together to figure out what to do when Hitler did whatever he was going to do next. A lot had happened since the summer. The Lindberghs were living in France then too, and they were invited along with a lot of important French people.

In the fall of 1938, we'd found a house in Paris, on the boulevard Suchet, close to the Bois de Boulogne, a substantial house that the French call a *palais* but that no Englishman would call a palace. It was a lot smaller than La Croë, but the Riviera had lost its charm for me and decorating a new house was a welcome distraction. My husband was with me constantly. He was keenly interested in furniture and Major Philips took an active part also. The fuss and bother and the constant decisions I had to make – colour schemes for the dining room and sitting rooms and my little boudoir, fabrics for furniture and windows, how much *chinoiserie* was chic and when too much of it began to look *nouveau riche* – took a lot out of me. I was trying for that crucial balance that Elsie Mendl believed in between freshness and *luxe*. It was all extremely wearing and demanding, the constant exercise of critical taste is exhausting, and I was so absorbed in it all that I did not learn about Mr Chamberlain's trips to Munich until one morning my husband told me there was a huge dust-up in Parliament and Duff Cooper had resigned from the Cabinet. That was in September or October, I'm not sure. Chamberlain went to Germany several times, I believe, and the final trip was the last straw for Duff.

In December, to Boysy's great joy, we were able to have Christmas in our own house. On Christmas morning, he clasped a Cartier double leopard head bangle[2] round my wrist and I burst into tears, and he wept too. 'We're so lucky, my precious angel,' he said. 'So happy at last to have our own wee Christmas by our own wee hearth fire. This is the best Christmas of my life.'

New Year's Eve was no better. He surprised me with another leopard, this one playing with a huge sapphire, round and blue like a globe,[3] like the globe Ribbentrop stole. 'See the little pussy-cat sitting on top of the world?' he said. 'Without a care in the world. That's how I feel, my darling.' My reaction to my Christmas leopards showed him how much I truly loved him, he said, and he would shower me with dear little kittens forever after. In a crazy way, I did want them. Sometimes I wore them on my nightgown.

But about the dinner. There were lots of American diplomats, and French officials, and the Lindberghs, who were living in Brittany near some French couple with batty ideas about science and magic.[4] The theme of the evening seemed to be solidarity with the Poles. An attractive young man, not strictly handsome but very charming, Gaston Palewski, paid a lot of attention to Anne Lindbergh. He became Nancy Mitford's lover when he was in London with de Gaulle, so I guess the French must have rated him high and trusted him with important assignments.

I made a point of standing close enough to hear what they were saying. They were talking about race, one of the many subjects Charles Lindbergh thought he knew all about. Palewski, who was dark and intelligent-looking, was urging Anne to examine these ideas critically. His words, not mine. The ideas about racial purity that she'd picked up on her travels were not reasonable. Her own

Chapter Twelve

country was a Melting Pot and doing very well. His family came from Poland, and no one was more French than he was, by education and culture. What they called *formation*. Napoleon himself came from Corsica, Palewski said. Yes, indeed, I thought, so he did. And his great Marshals, Ney, Kléber, and Masséna, came from many different places. France had Celts in Brittany, where she was staying, Germans and Italians in the east, Basques, Catalans, and Spaniards in the Pyrenees. Strength came from *complementarity* – his word again – from mixing, from living together and learning from each other. Anne said no, she thought being close to the earth made people strong, and that countries with lots of farmers did well.[5]

Palewski bowed over her hand at that point, defeated, I guess, and looked to his hostess, who shortly swept up with a pretty girl from Bryn Mawr doing her junior year abroad. She was introduced as the daughter of a senator. 'Which state, mademoiselle?' Palewski asked.

'A swing state,' she said. 'Daddy said I was to pick your brain about Danzig.'

'Gdansk,' he said. 'Let us use the city's Polish name.'

'I'm all ears,' she replied with a smile.

Men continued to buzz round Anne like bees around a flower, chatty bees, bees with a lot to say for themselves. One of the most attentive was an old Frenchman called Pierre Comert, who was in the Cabinet and friendly with the man Palewski worked for, Paul Reynaud,[6] a tough old bird, very anti-German. Duff told me all about them when he came to Paris in the spring. They were Radicals, and some called them Reds, but they were not Communists. It was the French Revolution, not the Bolshevik one, that they cared about, and they cared about it very much. M. Comert talked to Anne for a long time, and at one point he said, in a sort of public voice, or so it could be heard by many more people than Anne, that her late father, Dwight Morrow, was a great and good and wise man. 'I loved your father,' he said. 'I was proud to be his friend, and today some would consider him a Red.'[7] Such praise for her father, without a single kind word about the husband she expected everybody to idolise and fuss over, embarrassed the child. She flushed very pink, excused herself, and walked quickly across the room to where Mrs Kennedy was standing, talking to Lindbergh himself. They seemed well acquainted.

I chatted with Mrs Kennedy myself that evening, and I must say, she did not look bad for the mother of nine children. People joked that seeing Rose Kennedy made you believe in the stork. She was wearing a dress by Molyneux, more matronly than Mainbocher but well-made and becoming to her. She told me, in our brief conversation, that she liked Patou also.[8]

She was a cool one, I will say that for her, because during dinner her husband began the most awful rant about the way public opinion in the United States was being controlled and manipulated to drag them into a European war. The Jews and upper – class Yankees between them controlled damn near everything, radio, movies, newspapers, magazine and book publishing, and all the so-called elite colleges. Their oldest son, Joseph P. Kennedy, Jr., and a nicer, smarter, more athletic boy never lived, would you believe the coach kept him out of the Yale game so he wouldn't get his varsity letter? But that was not the worst of it. 'My son,' he said, not 'our son,' and Rose smiled sweetly, 'graduated from Harvard in June, and I thought it was high time for them to give me an honorary degree. I'm a Harvard man.[9] I'm a multi-millionaire. I've had a bunch of important political jobs and done 'em damned well. I put on a hell of a lot of pressure. Had a lot of people make a lot of calls. But some pompous old Brahmin put the kibosh on it.'

The lady sitting next to him smiled sweetly too. 'How sad, Your Excellency. How terribly disappointing. I can imagine how you felt, but perhaps another time. You and Mrs Kennedy have other children, haven't you?' This was such an understatement that several people laughed out loud.

Chapter Twelve

Kennedy continued, 'You know who they gave one to?'

The lady with the nice manners said she did not. Her daughter was Class of '38 too, they had that in common, but Radcliffe held its commencement on Wednesday, the day before Harvard's.

'Damned if they didn't give an honorary degree to the Governor General of Canada. Lord Tweedsmuir. John Buchan, who wrote all those books glorifying the Brits in the Great War.'[10]

'My children loved his books,' she said, 'And so do I.'

'He's nothing but a propagandist and a warmonger, and none too subtle. At commencement he talked about Lincoln and Shakespeare and the love of liberty that unites all English-speaking people. Wasn't love of liberty drove the Black and Tans.'

'There is a great deal of injustice in the world. No one would say there isn't,' she replied, all kind and fair and ladylike. 'It's our job to make sure there is not soon a great deal more.' I never found out who she was. She was a type I recognised, a goody-goody, and I never liked them, but in some situations they are exactly what you need.

Kennedy ignored her. He knew the type too and obviously didn't like it at all. He changed the topic from Harvard to Hollywood. 'I know a lot of film people. I know the stars from top to bottom.' This came as news to no one and a few looks were exchanged. Mrs Kennedy herself did not bat an eye while he boasted about how tight he was with the whole crowd, writers, producers, directors, actors, leading ladies, starlets. 'Even I can't get them to stop banging the drum for war and making movies about how great France and England and China are. Book publishing's worse. They gave the Nobel Prize this year to that *Good Earth* dame, the one who's so crazy about China.'

Throughout all of this, Mrs Kennedy listened and smiled. She could have been a plaster saint.

'Now this broad's done a hatchet job on Chuck,'[11] which it turned out was his pet name for Lindbergh. 'What's the word for it, Rosie, a Roman something?'

'*Roman à clef*,' she said. She told me that she felt perfectly at home in Paris – a Sacred Heart school drilled a considerable amount of French into its pupils.

'Makes him look like a fool,' Kennedy said. 'And it was printed as a serial in *Good Housekeeping* magazine, so damn near every woman voter in America read it, not just the lah-di-dahs in the book clubs. You can't tell me there's not a conspiracy.'

Anne Lindbergh interrupted him before he could say another word. 'I have read the book, dear Joe, if I may call you that. I feel we're really friends, and the only true thing in it is that people need the hope and inspiration heroes give them. No one could think for one moment that the protagonist is supposed to resemble my husband. He is a mountain climber, not a pilot. He has no children.' Well, she had a point there. If people knew one thing about Lindbergh, it was that his child had been kidnapped. Anne's eyes got teary, but she did not stop. 'He is intemperate and, what is if anything more unthinkable than that, he is unfaithful to his wife. What I found most distressing, if it were supposed to be us, which of course it obviously couldn't be and isn't, but if it were, is that the protagonist's wife, well, she has dark hair and tries to write poetry' – she blushed to the roots of her own dark hair –'his wife is supposed to have feelings for another man, a writer, a man of the Left. Imagine. And what is more ridiculous, a man who does nothing, nothing at all, but write, when she is married to a man who has really done things, wonderful, brave, difficult things.'

I saw a thought light up the intelligent face of Gaston Palewski. A flash of inspiration seemed to take hold of him and he looked as if he'd had a very good idea. I'm no intellectual myself, but I firmly believe there is no substitute for brains in a man. A man can't be really attractive if he is stupid.

Anne Lindbergh had brought an end to Kennedy's after-dinner speech, but it was quite a performance. Lindbergh said Joe was right: there was an active conspiracy to drag the United States into another European war and Roosevelt himself was the spider at the

Chapter Twelve

centre of the web pulling the strings and as guilty as sin. Thank God, the American people would never stand for a third term.

At that point the hostess stood up and said that the embassy belonged to the American people, not to any party or faction, and that electoral politics could not be discussed at its dinner table. People didn't linger after that and most of the guests left, but not before the four of us, Boysy and I and Anne and the Colonel, had a cosy chat.

My husband and the Man of the Year had a perfect meeting of the minds, such as they were, about how much they hated the press and how difficult it was to have any private life at all, hounded by such vultures and jackals and hyenas. The press misrepresented one's beliefs and made crude parodies of one's actually very deep thoughts and profound insights. Lindbergh did most of the talking and the Duke most of the nodding. He did say, 'Absolutely, old man,' when Lindbergh complained about the vicious attacks they both suffered simply because they spent time in Germany.[12]

The Lindberghs had been back in the fall, evidently, and Göring gave Lindbergh a medal, some sort of special German eagle. I asked if it was made of diamonds – you can always have them reset – and Anne said, 'Heavens, no, a diamond eagle, what an idea! It was just a medal, and Charles has been criticised for accepting it. But it's an immense honour, for service to mankind, not political in the least. Henry Ford is the only other American to get it.'[13]

Boysy said they hadn't given him any medals when he was there. He was hurt and I knew he'd fret about it for days. I was sorry the subject had come up.

Anne said we had so much in common that we must see more of each other. We would make a perfect little *partie carrée*, which is what the French call a double date. My husband asked her for her telephone number and I felt I had to invite them to our new *palais*.

There is an English bookshop on the rue de Rivoli, which is where Boysy bought the books he liked about upper-class Brits foiling gangs of evil foreigners. I sent my maid out first thing next morning to get Pearl Buck's book about Lindbergh. It's called *Other Gods*, and it's the only book I've ever read from cover to cover in one day. I had lunch on a tray in my boudoir and passed up dinner with Eugène and Kitty at Tour d'Argent, where they'd just named a new duckling dish after one of his cousins, *caneton Elie de Rothschild*. I had to finish it.

It was clear from the first page the book was about Lindbergh. Sure, he climbs a mountain instead of flying a plane. The point is that he's a 'mechanic',[14] as Nicolson said.

Miss Buck uses the word 'sullen' about eighty-five times in the first couple of chapters to describe the man, and 'stubborn' almost as often, and if that isn't Charles Lindbergh, I don't know who else it could be. He's also ignorant, with a mind 'totally uneducated, of course, and yet somehow needing no education in its unconscious self-sufficiency.'[15] I underlined this with a mascara pencil.

The hero, Bert Holm (Scandinavian like Lindbergh), dislikes the Chinese and he is rude to them. This from the 'dame who's crazy about China', so I assumed it was just about the most damning way the author could show what a prejudiced and provincial person he was. She doesn't give him as many crackpot ideas as Lindbergh actually had. I suppose nobody would believe it about a character in a book. They say truth is stranger than fiction, but she does put in the stuff about 'improving the race'. The character gets drunk at a dinner party and tells some silly debutante who tells a gossip columnist that the government should make the poor use birth control.[16] It was a great book and I couldn't put it down.

I thought Miss Buck was very smart about the way she handled the trip to Germany. She lumps Hitler and Mussolini together. I'd only met one of them, and I don't know if she'd met either one. I guess she must have met Chiang Kai-shek and his wife. She has this oaf Bert Holm 'hankering to see those two big fellows over there that are running the show. I'd like to know how they got on top the way they have.'[17] *I'd like to know how they got on top the way they*

Mrs Ernest Simpson, presented
at Court, June 10, 1931

HRH Edward, Prince of Wales,
Colonel in the Welsh Guards

Sir Harold Nicolson

Duff Cooper, 1st Viscount Norwich

William Somerset Maugham

George Andrew McMahon (Jerome Bannigan) apprehended July 16, 1936, in alleged attempt to assassinate Edward VIII

The King, Wallis Simpson and Katherine Rogers
ashore during the cruise of the *Nahlin*

Count Galeazzo Ciano, Shanghai, 1932

Colonel and Mrs Lindbergh with Hermann Göring, Karinhall, July 28, 1936

The Duke of Windsor, Schloss Enzesfeld, December 1936

FIFTEEN CENTS

January 4, 1937

TIME

The Weekly Newsmagazine

Dorothy Wilding

WOMAN OF THE YEAR
The Archbishop of Canterbury: "Truly this has been wonderful."
(See FOREIGN NEWS)

Volume XXIX

Number 1

Woman of the Year, *Time* magazine, January 4, 1937

The Duke and Duchess of Windsor on their wedding day, June 3 1937

The Windsors with Adolf Hitler, Berchtesgaden, October 1937

Count Ciano and Joachim von Ribbentrop, Munich, October 1938

George VI and Queen Elizabeth, guests of President and Mrs Roosevelt, with the president's mother, Hyde Park, June 1939

Sumner Welles and Joseph P. Kennedy, London, March 1940

The Duke of Windsor, Governor-General of the Bahamas and the Duchess

have! Well, I bet Charles Lindbergh would give his eye teeth to know that. Miss Buck could just as well have written 'DANGER' in big red letters on the page. In the book, though, his wife's father, rich and influential, is still living and the publicity agent he's hired to keep his son-in-law in line doesn't let him go.

As Anne said, and it was true, the hero in the book had faults that her hero didn't have. He was a drunk and a lecher. The real Lindbergh didn't seem to enjoy eating or drinking. He kept poor Anne constantly pregnant, but I never got the impression that making love was his idea of a good time.[18] Or that he liked women very much. Or men either. He was the 'Lone Eagle' after all.

There are some men – you know it when you see them, you know it right away, that they expect men and women to enjoy each other, that sex is important to them, they like it and they know you like it too. Gallo was more like that than any man I'd ever met. Lindbergh was just the opposite.

Spring came and bad things were happening everywhere and people began to talk about how beautiful the summer of 1914 had been. Duff, now out of the Cabinet, came to Paris often, meeting, I suppose, with the pro-war people, who were all his friends. He came to see me at the boulevard Suchet and we went for a walk in the Bois de Boulogne. It was May, and everyone knows what the Bois is like in May. I rather hoped he'd make love to me. He was nice and I liked him and my husband was away at Verdun, the scene of some big battle in the Great War, to give another speech in favour of peace at any price. 'Peace is a matter too vital for our happiness to be treated as a political question . . . in modern warfare victory will lie only with the powers of evil. Anarchy and chaos are the inevitable results, with consequent misery for all . . .'[19] I saw the script on his desk before he left. I think Charles Bedaux must have written it. Boysy could no more have done it himself than fly to the moon, and he didn't ask my help as he usually did when he was struggling to express himself. Anyway, he was off at an old battlefield and I was alone with Duff, who was chivalrous not amorous that day.

He told me nothing had surprised him that spring except the Italian invasion of Albania. He gave me a questioning look.

'I never even heard of Albania,' I said. 'I get it confused with Armenia.'

He told me that he'd known it was simply a matter of time before the Germans took all of Czechoslovakia as they'd done in March. He resigned last fall because he knew they could not be appeased. If they got the part they claimed was German, they would take the rest sooner rather than later. 'Some fools think they want security, but they are possessed. They are driven by appalling appetites.'

'Nobody who's seen them can think they want peace, but they don't think they'll have to fight,' I said. 'They think they can just take whatever they want because England and France are weak and cowardly.'

'They've no reason to think anything else. It's interesting that you read them so truly. People say that women instinctively seek peace, but I believe women are wiser than that. I know five happily married couples who disagreed about Munich, and in every case it was the wife who opposed appeasement. I shall now add you, my dear, and the Duke, to that honour roll. If I live to write a memoir, I shall mention it, without names, of course.'[20]

'Duff,' I said, 'what will Italy do?'

'I don't know. I've always believed the Axis could be split, though there's little hope for that now.'

'Count Ciano fears Hitler will invade Russia.'

'God willing,' Duff said. 'It may be the only thing that saves us. The Soviets are hard to read,' he said, sounding as if they really did puzzle him. 'I wish I knew what to make of Stalin replacing Litvinov, who's a delightful fellow, with Molotov. The new Foreign Minister's a thug. Are you still in touch with the Count, my dear?'

'No.'

Chapter Twelve

'That may be the best proof of how much he cares for you,' Duff Cooper, the kindest man I ever met, said to me in his gentle voice as we walked beneath the blossoming trees.

'He told me he read a book you wrote,' I said, 'and gave it to Mussolini, but he didn't like it.'

'You don't say? Must have been my *Talleyrand*. Did he mention anything in particular that struck him?'

'That treason might become the duty of a patriot.'[21] Gallo talked a lot that afternoon and I wasn't really listening because I didn't want to waste what little time we had in conversation. But it was such a funny thing for him to say that I remembered.

'Good gracious. Really? Let's hope he didn't mark that passage in the copy he gave Il Duce.' Duff drew my hand through his arm in a gesture that reminded me of Gallo and held it tight for a minute. 'Tough times ahead, my dear. History will ask a great deal of us all.'

We walked around one of the little lakes in the Bois. Neither of us spoke for some time. 'You seeing much of the Lindberghs?' he asked after a while.

'Not as much as the Duke wanted to,' I said. 'Lindbergh thought he was a bore and he's such a boor himself that he couldn't be civil, even to Hitler's favourite duke. We had them to dinner once with the Rothschilds, not a very jolly evening,[22] and he went home almost immediately afterwards to keep the United States out of the war. Anne followed with the children last month.'

Anne was at home, busy with her children and her writing, and one day I got a breathless letter from her, if letters can be breathless. Gaston Palewski's bright idea, it seems, was Antoine de Saint-Exupéry, a pilot almost as famous as her husband and a thousand times better in ways that should be obvious to any woman and especially to her. His writing spoke to her like none other, she said. He felt about flying exactly as she did, and her New York publisher, knowing of her admiration for his work, asked him to write the preface for her new book, and *he had agreed*. I could see why men like Kennedy and Lindbergh thought there was a conspiracy to create sympathy for France and England. Anne never dreamt politics was involved in this. 'Dearest Wallis,' she wrote. 'Can you believe that M. de Saint-Exupéry is actually coming to New York and that I am actually going to meet him? I may even manage to get him to stay with us for a few days.' She did not underline every word and she did not use a dozen exclamation points, but she sounded, poor child, like a girl at boarding school waiting for some heart-throb to show up with the tennis team from Andover. She must have been as lonely and desperate as I was. She certainly didn't sound like a happily married woman.

Coco Chanel told me that Saint-Exupéry was the most irresistible man in France. He descended from the most ancient provincial *noblesse*. His mother was intellectual and religious and kept her children close to the earth and close to peasants and artisans, *racinés*. He had a wide circle of friends to whom he was passionately loyal. In France, aviation was very much a 'career open to talent', and he had no racial or social prejudices. Women adored him and he responded, loving them seriously, more than one at a time but not promiscuously, she said. '*Mon Dieu*, Wallis, forget I said that. My English fails me sometimes.'

I shrugged. 'I don't ask for fidelity.'

'He's known for falling in love. He's recently married for the first time, a South American, tempestuous, some say, difficult. He's said to be fond of his mistress too. He's probably too honourable to seduce the wife of his host. I predict *une amitié amoureuse* that will knock her out.'

When Duff Cooper heard about it, he said it was a *coup de maître* and whoever thought of it should get the *Croix de Guerre* and be elected to the *Académie française*. 'If Saint-Exupéry can't convince her the civilisation that produced him is worth saving, no one can.'

Chapter Thirteen

"Marie-Ange," my manicurist, told me Napoleon invaded Poland and had an affair with a beautiful countess, the Countess Walewska, who was the mother of the only one of his sons who amounted to anything.[1] The child of the *vache Austrichienne* was a sickly little boy killed by his wicked Hapsburg uncles. The Austrians were not to be trusted even with blood relatives. She didn't predict Hitler would have any affairs in Poland. *On dit, mais madame la duchesse sait ce que l'on dit de sa virilité.* She told me that both Ribbentrop and Ciano had gone hunting in Poland, in some wild forest on the Russian frontier, with a Countess Potocka.

This interested me very much, but that was all she knew. I was prepared to be patient. I told her that the shade of nail polish she'd just put on wouldn't do. I wanted something lighter for the summer, a softer pink with a hint of peach. She'd have to start all over again. She said she'd have to charge me again and I agreed. It turned out she knew nothing more. She read in some gossip magazine that both of the men had been there and she didn't remember if they'd been there together or separately. In the end, I spent another hour and another fifty francs to learn more than I wanted to know about the Countess Walewska and the son who was a credit to her and to France, like Gaston Palewski, I gathered, more French than the French, and nothing whatsoever about the Countess Potocka.

We were leaving Paris the next day for La Croë, and I told Marie-Ange I wouldn't need her until early October when we returned to the boulevard Suchet. She looked at me as if I had not heard a word she said. 'Madame has not understood?' she said. 'We will be at war in the fall. May God protect you, madame, and all of us, and France.'

Cookie and George VI were expecting war too. They were in Washington, where no reigning British monarch had ever been. The Queen was almost as big a hit there as she was in Paris. Then they went to the President's summer house and ate hot dogs and sat on the porch with President and Mrs Roosevelt and his aged mother. For all I know, it may have been the first time Eleanor and Franklin ate wieners themselves, but it was a great picture for the purpose. Cookie looked very nice in a short summer frock with just two strands of pearls and a gardenia and quite a smart hat. Mrs Roosevelt was dressed for an Edwardian garden party in a full-length sprigged floral gown – the fabric could have been used to upholster a sofa – and a straw hat topped with flowers and bows. It did not become her, but it was welcomed as an expression of support for England. She generally looked like a poor woman waiting in line at a soup kitchen, not like the lady who ladled out the soup, so if she made that kind of effort, England must be important to her. They corresponded after that, Mrs Roosevelt and the Queen, and it looked like both the Roosevelts were getting ready to join the fight.[2]

Coco Chanel stayed with us while the King and Queen were in the States, and she was certain there would be war. Nothing rattled her. She would take what came and she talked quite frankly about what she planned to do if the Germans took Paris. 'I'll try to find someone reasonably presentable, not a madman, so that I can continue to do business.' Later, when people accused her of collaboration, she joked that a woman close to sixty doesn't ask to see a man's passport if he wants to make love to her. To me, she made plain she planned to please herself. 'I am Coco Chanel,' she said. 'I have refused dukes. I will make my choice.' She had vast experience of men, which she offered to me as we sat by the pool at La Croë. 'I do not understand this fascination with pilots, though I wish Saint-Exupéry good fortune in America. Some are full of fun and adventure, but not all. Lindbergh is not attractive. Göring, when he could still fit into the cockpit of a plane, was highly

Chapter Thirteen

decorated in the last war. He cannot have been pleasant company even then. The so-called good regiments contain too many imbeciles from families who have not had a brain among them for centuries. The best men are found in the Alpine regiments,' Coco said, and few Frenchmen know as much about wine as she knew about men.

'Are they equally good? All of them?'

'*Chacun à son goût*,' Coco said. 'But I assure you ours are the best, *les chasseurs des Alpes*, though one mustn't be chauvinist. The *Alpenkorps* are a cut above any other German I've ever met, and the *Alpini* are adorable, as one would expect.'

That summer was beautiful, and by then everyone was comparing it to the summer of 1914. There were, or so we heard very much second- or third-hand, 'flurries' of diplomacy. The French and British were trying to talk to the Russians. There was endless gossip about Italy. We had lunch with the American consul in Nice and I saw a copy of *Time* with Edda Ciano on the cover,[3] a cartoon, not flattering like the portrait they had of me. I slipped the magazine into my handbag and read the article when I got home. *Time* said she was pro-German and goading her father to go to war, and that her husband, the Foreign Minister, was less enthusiastic but his views would not prevail. The caption under her picture said that she wore the 'diplomatic trousers' in the family. There had always been rumours that she liked Germans more than she should. *Chacun à son goût*, maybe, but this was hard to believe.

We got the BBC on the radio and I took to listening to it. They reported that Gallo went to Salzburg in early August and had meetings with Hitler and Ribbentrop and returned to Rome.[4] There was no communiqué and nobody seemed to know if anything was decided.

August was Ribbentrop's month. He and the new Russian Foreign Minister, the one Duff said was a thug, made a deal to split Poland. The Molotov-Ribbentrop Pact it was called, and people still call it that, not the Stalin-Hitler Pact, though from what people tell me, neither one of them let their underlings do much on their own. It was a thunderbolt. Boysy, needless to say, was more shocked than I had ever seen him, unable to speak for half an hour and then sputtering with rage. 'I cannot believe Hitler capable of such a thing. How could he deal with such a bloody – I beg your pardon, my angel, I mean it in the literal sense, covered with blood – a tyrant whose hands are stained with the blood of so many innocent victims. And Ribbentrop! A gentleman who speaks perfect English, so attentive to you, my darling, so courteous, so considerate of your delicacy. Everyone knows he's in love with you, but his conduct has been beyond reproach. I never resented his feelings for you. I felt sorry for him. He can't help loving you, poor chap. I would not have believed him capable of such a thing.'

Percival Dreggs, who'd heard the news, came to join us on the terrace. He took a rather different view. 'There may be a reason, sir. You ought not to condemn the Germans without hearing their side of the story. The Italians may have let them down. Hitler may feel he has nowhere else to turn. The Poles are provoking him, sir, asking for trouble, you might say.'

'You think so?'

'I think you should await events, sir, and do nothing rash.'

'Damn, I will do something right now. I'll send them both telegrams.' My husband, the statesman.

'Molotov and Ribbentrop, sir?'

'Certainly not. I will have nothing to do with the Bolsheviks. I'll send telegrams to Hitler and to the King.'

'You might just call your brother, sir. I am sure in these difficult days he would be glad to hear your voice. It might be wise, at this moment, to attempt a reconciliation.'

'Dreggs, you cretin.' He was angrier than I'd ever seen him. 'I will write to Hitler and to Victor Emmanuel. He has treated me rather shabbily in the past, but I will overlook it. This is not a time for personal pettiness. I'll telegraph to the Führer and to the King of Italy. That should make an impression, don't you think?'

'Your Royal Highness.' Dreggs looked very, very nervous. 'You cannot sign them "Edward VIII R I". They'll stop your allowance.' That would have meant disaster for our household, and I saw how much poor Percival feared it.

'I will sign them "David", as I am known to my friends,' the Duke said, rather huffily. He may have told Hitler to call him that during their chats at Berchtesgaden. Victor Emmanuel, on the other hand, wouldn't know who 'David' was, but then, he wasn't calling the shots in Italy at the moment.

'Are you going to address him as King and Emperor?' I asked.

'You raise an excellent point, my precious love. What would you advise?'

'I'm not sure, darling. I leave politics and diplomacy to you.'

'I'll address him as my brother.'

'That might be taken by some, sir, if I may say so, to suggest that you regarded yourself in some sense as a, so to speak, sir, a, uh, that is to say, a monarch, sir, and they might cut off your allowance.'

' "Your Majesty", ' I said, ' "and my brother in Christ". He's Catholic.'

'Brilliant, fantastic,' Lightning Brain said. 'What a woman! What a queen.'

In the end, Victor Emmanuel did not need to figure out who sent the telegram. It was intercepted and published in a newspaper in Nice. Both the French and the Italian Rivieras were crawling with spies and you did need to be careful.

Hitler replied first, and the little man who was in charge of the post and telegraph pedalled out to our villa and woke us up to read a telegram from Berlin. Hitler said if war came, it would be England's fault. Victor Emmanuel replied later. Whether he got the telegram or read about it in the newspaper, I've no notion. He said that he'd do all in his power to preserve the peace and to keep Italy neutral if war broke out, and he joined his brother in prayer that this tragedy might yet be averted.[5]

Hitler invaded Poland, as everyone expected. England and France declared war, as maybe Hitler did not expect, and the Italians did not join in. My husband thought his letter was responsible for this and he was tremendously proud of himself. He thought we should stay at La Croë, close to Italy, because his diplomacy had been so effective. This was not the view in London, and emissaries were sent to inform us that we, unwelcome in the past, were now urgently requested, ordered you might say, to come home. They gave me very little time to pack and I did the best I could. We drove north, retracing the route I'd taken when I left in 1936, and it felt strange. Dickie Mountbatten and Randolph Churchill, Winston Churchill's son, met us and took us across the Channel in a Royal Navy destroyer.[6]

I greeted Dickie as an old friend. I always pretended I'd known him and his wife since their honeymoon in Washington in the twenties,[7] but I hadn't really met them then. They had fabulous glamour and I didn't move in those circles at that time. I'd no more known Dickie and Edwina than Marie-Ange knew Napoleon, but they played along – either because they'd met so many forgettable Americans they honestly couldn't recall if they'd met me or because they would not offend my husband by contradicting the 'woman he loved.' Mountbatten was not very gracious on this occasion, however, very grumpy about all my parcels. I had packed up everything valuable in our house, and much of what we had was valuable. I don't know what *impedimenta* means, but I know it's not good.

Cheering crowds failed to greet us in England and I saw no signs that the police were keeping them away. We were whisked away from Southampton to Fruity Metcalfe's country house, where we waited for word from the King or his ministers.

Eventually my husband was summoned to Buckingham Palace to see his brother. No invitation was extended to me by any member of his family to go anywhere. He was offered an office job in Wales, where, no doubt, much remained to be done, but he refused to stay in Britain if they wouldn't receive me at Court, and

I didn't look forward to Cardiff even after being allowed to curtsy to Cookie.

A few days later, the Secretary of War sent for Boysy and ordered him to report to the British liaison group attached to the French General Staff. It was not a pleasant meeting. The man was drunk with power, he said, an over-educated Jew who'd been a great swell at Oxford. He refused him, the Duke of Windsor, the rank of Field Marshal and said he couldn't even carry a baton. Far worse, he forbade him to take me, his wife, the Duchess of Windsor, with him when he visited the troops. 'He had the impertinence to say he feared there would be disturbances, particularly in Scotland.'

'I don't care,' I said. And I didn't.

'I was more than a match for him, though,' Boysy said. 'I wore him down and in the end he agreed I could wear all my decorations on my battle dress.'[8]

'That's marvellous, darling. You put him in his place.' And back we went to the boulevard Suchet.

Poland fell quickly to the Nazis and the Russians took the eastern half, including, people said, a big forest with boars and bison and a kind of black and brown zebra. I thought it must be the forest where Gallo hunted with the Polish countess. I asked people if there were any great cats, but there aren't, except for the lynx.

I was happy to be back in Paris. France was at war, but nothing was happening. People called it the 'phony war' and the *drôle de guerre*, and cynical people called it the 'bore war'. Everyone was edgy. My masseuse's son was on the Maginot Line, and Marie-Ange wanted her boyfriend to marry her before he was killed. She grew more and more insistent about this and her reason became more and more apparent.

It was a very ordinary rainy Paris winter. My husband, like every other man and woman on active service, got a Christmas card from the Queen, a photo of her in a diamond tiara, diamond necklace, and diamond ear-rings.[9] All very pure and shining bright. I was beginning to dread Christmas and I may have dropped a hint or two that I had enough leopards for the moment. My present was, if anything, worse. My husband gave me a sapphire necklace with nine flower heads, eight more than on my dear old chalcedony bead necklace. These were some *bijoux*. Cartier was definitely expecting *le déluge*. There were two rows of sapphire beads, hung with thirty-two diamond pendants, and each of the flowers was clotted with diamond dewdrops.[10] 'I thought you must be tired of your old sapphires, sweetie puss,' he said. 'You seldom wear them now, and blue is such a good colour for you, darling, you are my true blue best girl.' What can you do? I wore it on New Year's Eve and we toasted 1940, which was going to be a big year, with a presidential election in the United States that interested everyone very much.

Early in the New Year, Marie-Ange, now very *enceinte*, asked if she could present her husband to me when next she did my nails. I was curious, naturally, and said I'd be happy to meet him. Well, he turned out to be black as the ace of spades, a handsome devil of a Senegalese, Corporal Napoleon Amadou. I shook his hand and kissed her and wished them well.

My husband spent his time with the General Staff at Versailles or visiting front-line troops. As the winter wore on, he went less and less often to the front. From time to time I would hear him talking to himself, in French, which I knew he didn't speak, or hardly at all. I tried to catch what he was saying, and finally I made it out. He was saying, '*Laissez-moi passer, s'il vous plaît, je suis le prince de Galles.*' 'Let me pass, please, I am the Prince of Wales.'[11] He was made to memorise this, he said, before he was sent to France in 1916. He was not made to memorise any German phrases because that was the one foreign language he spoke and, in that war, if he'd been taken prisoner, the first officer who saw him would have passed him along to one of his German uncles. He was

Chapter Thirteen

tense, waiting for something to happen, and I got the distinct impression he knew what was coming. Everyone knew what was coming, of course, so I do not say he had anything from the horse's mouth, so to speak.

Duff and Diana Cooper came to Paris in March, back from the United States, where they'd been doing their bit. They were travelling with a man called Walter Lippman, who was close to Roosevelt.[12] Harold Nicolson was in France too. They said war was raging in the States between the interventionists and the isolationists, as they were called. Lord Tweedsmuir had died in Montreal in February. Most people think of Diana Cooper as frivolous, but she said the strangest thing. 'We needed him terribly. He believed in Divine Providence.' Duff said his posthumous book would help. Heaven helped those who helped themselves.[13]

Nicolson said Lindbergh was showing his true colours, making more and more outrageous speeches – bitterly anti-Semitic, full of anger and loathing about unseen forces that controlled the press and the means of influencing public opinion. He was associated with others as sullen as himself but not all as stupid: Henry 'History is bunk' Ford, and you can imagine what Harold Nicolson and Duff Cooper thought of him. Father Charles Coughlin, no longer on the radio but publishing a weekly newspaper. Some writers and publishers, but nobody first-rate. Alice Roosevelt and her long-time friend Senator Borah.[14]

I was surprised they were still together and I was able to provide some background. They all knew she was Teddy Roosevelt's daughter and a famous society hostess and wit. They wanted to know about her late husband. 'Nicholas Longworth was a charming man. I knew him slightly. He was a Harvard man and a thorough gentleman. Borah's a ruffian from the Wild West. He spent his youth brawling in saloons and people say he's been thrown out of every bordello in the Rockies.'

'Astonishing,' Diana said. ' "Crazy salad", as Yeats says. Whatever do intelligent women see in these preposterous desperadoes? Think how long that clever, charming woman in Milan – '

'Darling,' Duff said, and she caught his warning in midair and went on without missing a beat.

'Borah's from Idaho, isn't he?' she asked. 'The Mountain States seem intractably isolationist. Burton K. Wheeler's from Montana. We heard a lot about him too. He seems to be in touch with Kennedy. There are a lot of Irish in Montana, in the copper mines.'[15]

'Borah wants Lindbergh to run for President,' Duff said. 'But the Lone Eagle claims to be above politics. Men like that are always dangerous. Politics requires paying attention to the thoughts and feelings of other people. Claiming to be above politics means nothing more and nothing less than refusing to do that.'

'What about Anne?' She hadn't written to me for months, but everyone in the world knew she'd fallen madly in love with Saint-Exupéry because, in her innocent way, she talked and wrote constantly about how marvellous he was.[16] I was surprised, after all I'd heard about how crazy she was about him, that he had failed to convert her to the Allied cause.

'He'd been ordered to make sure of her,' Duff said. 'Reynaud says he simply couldn't do it. She's sentimental and surprisingly conventional and fragile, with several young children who need her. As those surely brutes tend to be, Lindbergh's a cruel and autocratic father. Saint-Ex feared she'd lose her mind if they became lovers, and he would not risk it.'[17]

'Lindbergh's *typiquement typique*,' Diana laughed. 'It really isn't funny, but it is:

> Behold, my child, the Nordic man
> And be as like him as you can.
> His legs are long; his mind is slow;
> His hair is lank and made of tow.
> Oh, what a lot of harm they do.

The last line's mine, not Belloc's,' she said.

That was the best poem I'd ever heard. I wondered if poor Anne knew it and if she'd ever tried to discuss it with Mrs Göring. 'Was that written about Lindbergh, like Pearl Buck's book?'

'That's a page-turner, isn't it?' Diana said. 'But this one antedates him by some years. It's called "The Three Races".'

'Darling,' Duff said. 'It's a foolish little poem, by no means his best work. 'Nuff said?'

She was caught up in the fun of the poem and continued: 'Hitler's not Nordic, of course, he's Alpine: Sallow and *chétif,* yellow, He is a most unpleasant fellow.'

'What about the others?' I asked.

'*Doucement, chérie,*' Duff said. '*Attention, sois sage.*'

'The most degraded of them all,' Diana said, with a great whoop of laughter. She was high-spirited and she really hated the Nazis.

> Mediterranean we call.
> His hair is crisp, and even curls,
> And he is saucy with the girls.[18]

'Oh,' I said. 'I see. Very funny.'

'The Nazis are demented about sex, don't you think?' Diana Cooper, happy, outspoken, sure of herself, daughter of a Duke, wife of a man who loved women and loved her best.

'I believe they are,' I said.

'That is a malicious slander,' Boysy said. 'Popularised by sinister interests who deliberately distort the Nazis' views in pursuit of their own, um, sinister interests, as I said.' There were more long words in this statement than he generally used. 'The Germans are quite properly concerned about the sanctity of the family and the purity of their women. During Weimar, the inflation, you know, it threatened many families, and money-lenders took advantage of women, even war widows. It was shocking.'

In April, the Germans attacked Norway and Denmark. After this, my husband signed a rather indiscreet letter about the English government: 'We shall have to purge ourselves of much of our out-of-date system of government.'[19] I don't know who wrote it, and when I asked him, he said he wrote it himself, which I am sure he didn't.

They struck Holland, Belgium, and France in May. They advanced very fast and were outside Paris in a matter of days, and my husband said he feared for my safety. I think he really did, so maybe he wasn't sure I'd be all right when they got there. He came home in the early afternoon of the sixteenth of May and told me I had only two hours to pack. He was taking me to Biarritz. Now, it is all very well to be devoted to your wife, but Boysy was supposed to be a major general on active duty. Some people criticised, and continue to question to this day, his decision to accompany me all the way to Biarritz.[20]

The roads were jammed with refugees, and he kept shouting, '*Je suis le prince de Galles, laissez-moi passer*.' We got to Evreux, to the Hôtellerie du Grand Cerf, and the innkeeper who had been so sweet about hiding my notes put us up in a tiny ground-floor room on two camp beds. We made it to Biarritz and the comfort and safety of the Hôtel du Palais, and there I found Kitty, cool as a cucumber, sitting in the lobby surrounded by luggage, holding her jewel case. Eugène was carrying a large leather portfolio, which, I suppose, held paintings and drawings they managed to bring with them from Austria.

'Kitty,' I said, 'how nice to see you. Where are you going?'

'Long Island,' she said. 'You must come to see us when we've settled in, next spring perhaps.'

Her kind invitation made my blood run cold. If even Kitty wasn't prepared to have us in the United States until after the presidential election, we were beyond the pale. My husband felt the same way. Back in Paris, when he returned to his post, no one talked to him or trusted him with the smallest task. On May 26 he asked, and got, leave to go to our house at Cap d'Antibes. He collected me at Biarritz and we journeyed once more across France to the Riviera.

I'd taken a subscription to the *New Yorker* because I'd hoped we could go there, and split our time between Manhattan and Palm Beach. I was afraid of the Germans. I was afraid they'd invade England after they conquered France and drag us back with them. I was sure the Brits would not welcome us with open arms. They'd be more likely to lynch us if we came back with the invaders. I could see us both, strung up in Trafalgar Square. The prospect terrified me. The woman who wrote the 'Notes from London' in the *New Yorker* kept reporting how brave and cheerful and determined everyone was. That must have been one of the magazines Lindbergh had in mind when he talked about the Jews and the pro-British elitist snobs controlling the press.

Duff was back in the Cabinet now. Chamberlain was out and Churchill was in and he made Duff Minister of Information, because they don't have a Minister of Propaganda in England. The British tried to drive the Germans out of Norway and it was a disaster and Duff told the people the truth. That woman got him exactly right: 'Mr Duff Cooper . . . inspires confidence because he tells his listeners without any nonsense that they're in for an extremely unpleasant time, in which he knows they're going to behave well.'[21]

I thought I was in for a perfectly ghastly time, and I wasn't sure how well I'd behave.

Chapter Fourteen

France surrendered, or some of it did, enough so that the Germans could set up a puppet government. There weren't any kings they could use, so they chose a hero from the last war. The English got out, early in June, with as many men and guns as they could get off the beach at Dunkirk. There was no fighting where we were until the middle of the month, when Italy declared war. We heard about it on the radio. Close as we were to the frontier, we hadn't heard a shot fired. Percival Dreggs paid the Italian gardeners their last week's wages and sent them home. Several asked to return in the *dopoguerra*.

The fourteenth of June was a beautiful day, as days generally are on that heavenly coast.[1] We kept the radio on most of the time and the cook, who was a character, had her own wireless set in the kitchen and she talked to it like a telephone. I was out on the lawn in the early evening, surrounded by a clutter of what Dickie Mountbatten called *impedimenta*, when I heard her shout, '*Venez, venez vite. C'est la reine qui nous parle.*' I'd been living in France now for more than three years, so I understood a little. She was saying, 'Come, come quick. The Queen is speaking to us.' She turned up the volume so it could be heard outside.

It was Cookie, sure enough, speaking from Buckingham Palace in French to the women of France. I went closer to hear what she was saying. I couldn't catch everything she said, but it was having a terrific impact on my maids. They were kneeling outside the kitchen window, some with their rosaries in their hands. The menservants were standing, heads bared. Her voice came on, clear and firm. Our cook joined the others outdoors. She kept crossing herself and repeating, '*Que Dieu vous bénisse, votre Majesté et monsieur votre mari, le bon roi.*'

'*Et les chères petites,*' one of the maids said, through her sobs. '*La belle Élisabeth qui s'appelle "Lilibet" et sa jolie petite soeur.*'

'*Les chères demoiselles, nos princesses,*' the cook corrected her.

The dear young ladies and our – our! – princesses. My God, and Shirley Temple had a nickname that French parlourmaids knew and I didn't. Of course, her parents would never have let her within three counties of me.

Cookie ended with, '*Vive la France!*'

'God Save the King' was played and then the Marseillaise.[2]

The men were crying now too, all of them. '*Vive la France! Vive la reine!*' People must have been shouting it all over France. I wondered if my masseuse had heard Cookie, or Marie-Ange.

It wasn't fair. I had to evacuate La Croë again, now that Italy might attack Nice any minute. I had spent the day packing up things I had just finished unpacking. Some of the larger pieces were still on the lawn. I broke my nails and scratched my hands with twine and my nose was red and itching with sawdust. There were *objets* I couldn't trust to servants who were fretting about their husbands and boyfriends, injured, missing, or taken prisoner. Not one of them really had her mind on her work, so it fell to me. I was a wreck. My hair and nails had not been done for a week, and there was Cookie, snug and smug in Buckingham Palace, swanning on the radio, showing off all the verbs she'd learned when she was twelve. She had the King of England, calm and cool and spruce in his nice naval uniform. I had a snivelling wreck, not sure if he should try to make it to Spain or Portugal or bolt over the closer mountains to Switzerland.

I walked to the end of the terrace to get away from the servants who were still praying and crying and embracing and cheering and singing on the lawn. I found Major Grey Philips of the Black Watch, standing at rigid attention with tears streaming down his cheeks. I never trusted him again.

'Thank God,' I said as I heard a rumble of thunder. 'Some rain will clear the air.' I didn't care if any of the things I'd left on the lawn got wet. What's another inlaid table more or less?

'Not thunder, ma'am. The RAF is bombing Genoa.[3] I hope those Fascist bastards get the licking they deserve. The swine. Holding back all winter and then stabbing France in the back when she's down.'

We left a few days later, on my birthday, the nineteenth of June, and went in caravan with some other English and Americans who had villas on the coast. I heard the Italians were stopped at Mentone, stopped by the *chasseurs des Alpes*. It must have been humiliating and I didn't like to think about it at all. I had plenty of other things to think about as we waited at roadblocks while Lightning Brain introduced himself as the *Prince de Galles*. We were held up for several days in Perpignan, which is close to the Spanish border, and at last, with a few more *Laissez-moi passer s'il vous plaît, je suis le prince de Galles*, we made it into Spain.[4]

Boysy had gathered, somewhere, a poor opinion of that part of Spain, and he thought we should leave Barcelona and make our way to Madrid as soon as possible, and in a way he was right, because we were received royally, so to speak. People were more than hospitable. We stayed at the Madrid Ritz, the best hotel, where lots of Germans were staying also, and the Spaniards would have given us a spare palace the minute we asked. I went to see one of them and it was very nice, with a sort of Arabian Nights look that would have been fun to make a bit more *chic* and modern.[5]

That was not to be either. We kept hearing from Churchill that Madrid was unsuitable and that the Duke must come home and join his brothers in the fight to save the world.[6] People expected that Hitler would invade England, across the Channel, as Napoleon thought about doing but never actually tried.

Speaking of Napoleon, I got a note from Marie-Ange, forwarded from our house in Paris. Sergeant Amadou, she wrote, was *mort pour la France*, and she was going with their baby to Dakar. Her mother-in-law, a schoolteacher, feared they wouldn't be safe in France. If the Germans saw a woman with a black baby, they'd assume she was a

Chapter Fourteen

prostitute. They'd never believe she was the widow of a non-commissioned officer or, if they did, they wouldn't care. Marie-Ange was afraid to live in Africa, but she was more afraid of the *Boches*, so she'd stay there until it was safe to come home. It would be safe to come home one day – the General said so and so did the Queen.

I told Boysy my manicurist wrote that she'd had a son.

'I suppose she wants money. That savage deserted her, I expect?'

'He didn't desert anyone. He died at Dunkirk, covering the British retreat.'

'So she says. She's probably ashamed to tell you the truth.'

'Would you like to know the baby's name?'

'Not particularly, my dear, but you'll tell me anyway. I suppose you can't help yourself. Wives always try to distract their menfolk from serious business with little bits of pointless gossip.'

He'd been spending too much time with the Germans in the bar at the Ritz. I could always tell when he got superior like that, and this was one bit of pointless gossip he ought to hear. 'She's calling him Charles de Gaulle Amadou, and they are going to live with his grandparents in Senegal.'

'Shocking,' he said. 'She'll probably have a dozen more in Africa.'

A German invasion of England seemed to be in the works. My husband was very popular in the Ritz bar, and, in London, they were getting ready for whatever came. There was talk of sending the princesses to Canada, and Cookie was widely quoted as saying that children should not be parted from their mother, and she would never leave her husband, and the King would never leave England.[7] She returned to London from Balmoral when the bombing started, and there were stories, endless stories, about what she said and did in East London. She came across a Cockney woman trying to get her dog out of the cellar of her ruined house, where he'd been howling and whimpering since the air raid began. People were afraid the house would collapse on him, and you know how the Brits are about their pets. Cookie told the woman she was 'rather good with dogs' and she bent down into the rubble and coaxed him out.[8] She was reported to be taking pistol practice every morning in the garden behind Buckingham Palace. She vowed not to be taken alive, and I thought that Ribbentrop was wrong, as he so often was, in thinking that queens did not know what the people wanted to hear.

The last straw for me was Harold Nicolson. I regarded this as a personal betrayal. After all, he'd fetched my notes back from Evreux in the fall of 1937 and I always felt I could rely on him. Harold Nicolson said, after all I'd done in Egypt, that Cookie was 'the greatest Queen since Cleopatra.'[9] With her sweet smile and her blue eyes and her rose-leaf complexion, she didn't look anything like that elegant bust in Berlin.

But I had worse troubles than Nicolson flattering Cookie. We were supposed to get back to England while it was still safe to cross the Channel. My husband refused to return unless I was received into the bosom of his family, and what a treat that would have been, and accorded a rank appropriate to my dignity and my irreproachable conduct. Norman Birkett may have not completely fooled the judge in Felixstowe, but Boysy had always believed I was pure as the driven snow[10] and, sad to say, I had never in the full technical sense of the word committed 'adultery' with him, as Gallo guessed. It made me sick to think about Genoa.

There were 'flurries of negotiations' over my title and my rank and where I could live and who would visit me, or, I should say, my husband kept making demands on my behalf that the King and his ministers kept rejecting. Boysy spent a lot of time talking to the Germans too, and to close Spanish friends of the Germans, and finally Churchill ordered him to leave Madrid. He put into words, something he was good at, the fear that the Germans might kidnap us, and he did it cleverly, not suggesting that the Duke would willingly help the Germans, but that the King and Queen Mary and all the loyal subjects of the King in Britain and the Dominions must be spared the sight of their former Sovereign in captivity. In the end he threatened my husband, who was, as I may have mentioned, a major general in the British army, with court martial if he did not return immediately to such duties as the War Office saw fit to assign. But he had already chased Boysy out of Madrid. We got this telegram in Lisbon.[11]

England has a lot of say in what happens in Portugal. Port wine comes from Portugal and the ties between the two countries go back a long way. We stayed in a villa owned by a banker called Ricardo de Espirito Sancto e Silva.[12] His name was sure to mean, Gordie said, that his family were Marranos, Jews forced to convert to Christianity at an earlier period who'd taken a name that advertised their new faith. He was a banker, after all, and he was also some kind of papal knight, I believe. I was never sure what titles he had.

Gordie – I should introduce him – was sent from London to keep an eye on us. He was an officer in the Black Watch, like Major Philips, and was in the Foreign Office before the war. George Arthur Henry Ireton Wellesley Wallingford-Just, called 'Gordie' or 'Willingly-Joust,' Duff wrote in a letter introducing him. Duff said I could trust him completely. He had a good mind and a good heart, and if Duff said that, I knew it must be true. Gordie said he was keen to learn Portuguese because he loved French and Italian literature, and Provençal and Catalan too, and he'd never had a chance to learn Portuguese, which he seemed to do in about two days.

I was glad he was there because, a week or so after we settled into the house of Senhor Holy Ghost, Ribbentrop flew into Lisbon dressed as a cardinal, the Catholic kind, not the bird, bright red head to toe, with a bouquet of seventeen matching roses. He came in clerical garb, he explained, so that he could enter Portugal inconspicuously. Gordie hooted when he heard that. 'The FO knows how many cardinals there are in the world and where they all are at any given moment. Standing orders since the time of Queen Bess.'

Ribbentrop begged audience with the Duke, who was still furious about his deal with Molotov and refused to see him. Ribbentrop then asked to see me. He said he had an important message from 'the second most important man in Rome' that he was sure would interest me.

I was staggered. I flew through the villa until I found Lightning Brain, playing solitaire in the library. I told him it was his duty to hear what Ribbentrop had to say, and it didn't take me too long because Boysy was curious himself. He seemed at loose ends since we left Madrid. The villa had a beautiful courtyard with lots of statues and fountains, where we sat, Boysy and I, and Gordie and Senhor Holy Ghost and Ribbentrop, drinking Madeira.

'I come,' he said, 'from Madrid, where I was furnished with this magnificent regalia. The clergy has been restored to its former glory in Spain. I do, however, in truth, have a message for Your Royal Highnesses from, as I confided to the most beautiful and fascinating woman in the world, the second most important man in Rome.'

'Very wrong of you, my good man, very coarse and vulgar,' Boysy interrupted him, and Ribbentrop looked as if he'd slapped him across the face. 'My good man,' as Ribbentrop knew, was what an English gentleman would have called a plumber come to see about a leaky pipe in the loo. He was, for once, speechless.

'The Bolsheviks have destroyed your manners and your sense of what is right and proper and the respect that is due to your superiors. I've had my differences in the past with the King of Italy.' He paused. He must have felt the slight to his brother monarch, because he seldom went on about anything so long. 'His Imperial Majesty, the Emperor of Abyssinia.' He was willing to throw that in too. 'But, in my presence, you cannot refer to the Sovereign of any country as its "second most important man".'

I couldn't listen to another second of Boysy's dithering. 'What did he say?' I asked, and my voice may have been a little shrill.

'His Holiness the Pope,' Ribbentrop announced, as if the man had just appeared before us, 'for it is His Holiness the Pope of whom I speak, Your Royal Highnesses. I meant no disrespect to His Imperial Majesty, your brother.'

'The Pope?' I dropped my wineglass and it shattered on the ceramic tiles. The butler rushed forward and knocked over the decanter and a heavy silver bowl that held Ribbentrop's roses. The bowl rolled into the nearest fountain, taking a marble cherub and a dolphin or two with it. For several minutes there was a big commotion, with servants rushing to and fro and an ugly gleam of pleasure in Ribbentrop's eye.

When things quieted down, he spoke. 'His Holiness entrusted me with a message, a gesture of remarkable charity. He is a truly Christian man.'

Boysy and I were, for once, equally baffled. 'Yes?' my husband said. 'I will hear it. Proceed.'

'His Holiness authorised me to assure you that if you converted to Catholicism, if both of you did, and also agreed henceforth to live as brother and sister, he would receive you at the Vatican. He would not insist that you took up residence in separate households. In time, after suitable penance, he might himself agree to bless your union. He judges that annulments would not be necessary because your first marriage, Your Royal Highness' – he bowed to me as he spoke –'took place in a Protestant church and the second in a registry, so neither would be regarded in canon law as a valid sacrament. He would be prepared to hear your confession.' Again he was talking to me, with a look in his eyes I cannot describe. 'He would be prepared to hear your confession personally.'

'Mighty white of him,' I said. I bet he'd like to hear my confession. Who could have put him up to it? It was the battiest thing I'd ever heard, and a little scary. I was surprised that my husband appeared to consider it.

'What do you advise?' he asked. 'You judge it would be helpful – ' He paused. 'Useful, say, with the Irish?'

'Conceivably,' Ribbentrop said. 'Pius XII is a most extraordinary man, as Her Royal Highness observes with her customary insight

into men's character and her infallible . . . *le mot juste* in this case!'
He laughed his hateful little laugh. 'Her *infallible* judgment of
men's trustworthiness and integrity. He is, in truth, a "white man".'
He lived in Germany for many years, as you know. I met his
companion, the little Bavarian nun. She is an angelic creature. She
sat on a footstool by his chair while we conferred and left us only to
prepare his hot chocolate, which he graciously vouchsafed me to
share. If I may offer a psychological insight, Your Royal Highnesses,
not a Freudian one, of course' – again he laughed his nasty laugh –'I
believe it is the purity of their love that enables him to imagine that
you might consent to live as he proposes. She calls him "Holy
Father" and he calls her "my child" and occasionally *Liebchen*.
Evil – minded people say evil things, as they will. He told me she
represents for him the heavenly purity of his beloved Bavaria before
it was corrupted by the serpent of the Munich Soviet.'

'I've heard he's an improvement on his predecessor,' [13] Boysy said.
I was surprised he knew one Pope from another. I certainly didn't.

'Incomparably so. Everyone agrees. Ambassador Kennedy, who
represented the United States at his investiture, has been his friend for
years.[14] Among my colleagues, even those, like Himmler, who most
embrace Teutonic neo-paganism believe they can work with him.' [15]

If Himmler likes the Pope, I thought, it was time to let bygones
be bygones with the Church of England. Did the Germans ask him
to find out about my sins? Or Edda, who liked Germans? Maybe
the Pope was just curious about me. A lot of men were.

'I always urge my colleagues not to alienate Catholics,' Ribbentrop said, and returned to the subject of Joe Kennedy. 'The shrewd
and genial American met the Foreign Minister of Italy at the
investiture of Pius XII and disliked him immediately. "Silliest man I
ever met and a pompous ass", Kennedy confided to me. He's a
proper Bostonian, for all his *bonhomie*. He was aghast to find a man
of Cabinet rank, even in a country so notoriously amoral, to be such
an open and unabashed libertine, revelling in orgies the like of
which even Rome had never previously seen.' [16]

Chapter Fourteen

I knew I had to let this pass. Gordie Willingly-Joust slew the dragon for me. 'Oh, come, sir, that's the pot calling the kettle black. It's a joke in London that American visas can be had for love or money but love's faster. Kennedy interviews all the pretty refugees in private. The embassy staff finally removed the sofas from his office after one of the tabloids called them "casting couches". They've been replaced with spindly Chippendale armchairs on loan from the Victoria and Albert.'

Senhor Holy Spirit asked Ribbentrop if Kennedy was going to Chicago for the Democratic Party convention and he said he didn't know. His eldest son was a delegate, however, and he was pledged to a candidate opposing Roosevelt.[17]

'Whatever happens at the convention,' Ribbentrop said, 'Roosevelt's days are numbered.' The President, he went on to say, sent some undersecretary to the four capitals, Berlin and Rome, Paris and London, and Kennedy's role in all this was merely to schedule his appointments with English officials.[18] The man did not draw upon Kennedy's vast knowledge of British politics, nor did he in any way consult him as a colleague and an equal in the formation of foreign policy. ' "A stuck-up snob", as the Ambassador so rightly said. I myself found him an ignorant fool[19] and completely indifferent to Germany's legitimate national interests and historic destiny.' Ribbentrop said Kennedy had discerned the problem: the man was not just a snob, he was part of the very inner circle of snobs, the Groton roommate of Eleanor Roosevelt's brother.[20] 'His Excellency is as alert to the dangers posed by hidebound reactionaries as we are. You cannot toy with impunity with a man like Joseph P. Kennedy. Roosevelt has made a dangerous enemy.'

'Sumner Welles,' Gordie said. 'You met him too?' That was all he said.

Ribbentrop could not contain himself. 'Very briefly,' he said. 'For a short time. My Italian counterpart was more fortunate. He met with Welles several times in February and March. That insufferable braggart no doubt assured him he was keeping Italy neutral – when they met alone, that is.[21] He would not have dared to flaunt his prowess in the presence of the *suocero di tutti suoceri*.'

Boysy asked Ribbentrop to stay for dinner. I excused myself. I couldn't have swallowed a bite and I wanted to be alone for as long as possible. The villa had a hundred bedrooms. Unfortunately, people assumed the lovers of the century would want to sleep together and I was almost never by myself. I lay awake for hours in our big bed, dreading Boysy's arrival, and finally I fell asleep. He must have talked with Ribbentrop half the night. I felt a hand on my shoulder and opened my eyes as the sky was just getting grey.

'Precious, what's a *suocero*?'

'You'll have to ask Ribbentrop. I can't speak Italian.'

'I don't like to ask him,' Boysy said. 'He acts as if I should understand everything he says and I can't, even when he speaks English. He talks too fast and he's always alluding to things. Not the most straightforward chap. I thought it might have to do with a secret society, like the Black Hand, some sinister outfit, with secret handshakes and oaths and passwords.'

'They were right at Oxford, darling,' I said. 'You do learn from life, not from books. Ask Gordie in the morning.'

At breakfast, Gordie said I had to see Ribbentrop again. It was important. I had to make him believe I liked him and I had to arrange to keep in touch with him.

I didn't see how I could do that after yesterday, but Gordie said Ribbentrop was obsessed and he'd give us an opportunity. 'Just follow my lead. You'll know what to do when the subject comes up. Be sure to ask him about Mme Chanel.'

And come up it did. The man himself, no longer dressed in scarlet but in a white linen suit and a rakish straw hat, came back, at Senhor Espirito Sancto's invitation, to see the villa's gardens. This was before lunch, and we were drinking wine on the terrace again. Mr Holy Ghost asked, in his capacity as a concerned Catholic layman, about the fate of the Church in Poland. 'We hear, and we thank Our Holy Saviour and His Blessed Mother, that the Countess Potocka has found sanctuary in the Eternal City.'

'Ciano's claiming credit for that too.'[22] Ribbentrop was obsessed. 'She escaped from the Russians, and that snake's taking the credit. Can you believe such shameless effrontery? Which of us, do you imagine, is closer to Molotov? Who negotiated with the Russians? Who consummated the deal of the century? Who, Ciano or I?'

Gordie led him on. 'There's a version of the story, sir, that the Russians turned her over to the Gestapo because they wanted you to take care of her and you tried to send her back, and while you were talking it over, she escaped. In any case, I'm sure she's grateful.'

This was my opening. 'I am sure the Countess is profoundly grateful to you, my dear old friend. And if you were a woman, Leff-tenant, you would know that a woman's instinct tells her, as Herr von Ribbentrop said yesterday, when she can trust a man, when her heart tells her to depend upon his chivalrous devotion and rely on his honour and discretion. When he is the sort of man, alas too rare, who places her honour above his own selfish pleasure. I am sure the Countess Potocka knows she owes her freedom to Herr von Ribbentrop, and she knows too that he, unlike some other men, would never ask anything in return.' I'd lived with the smart set for years and I can get on a high horse with the best of them if I need to. Ribbentrop looked as if somebody had just pinned a diamond eagle on his jacket. 'You are a true knight, dearest Jo, and I have long treasured your friendship,' I said, giving him my hand to kiss, for, I hoped, the last time. 'I wonder,' I said when he let go of my hand, 'if you know how Coco Chanel's doing? She's not the lady the Countess must be, but I've always liked her.'

Ribbentrop continued to beam. This was his lucky day. 'She is well. By a most extraordinary coincidence, she has formed a friendship with a friend of mine, stationed in Paris. Splendid fellow, old family, good blood.'

'Good regiment?' Boysy asked.

'*Alpenkorps*, originally. Detailed now for special assignment in Paris.'

Vive la France, I thought. 'How very nice,' I said. 'Perhaps you might be able to help me keep in touch with her, if I want her advice about fashion or need to order a new frock?'

Nothing could give him greater pleasure. He could always get word to her and, he added, she would always be able to get word to him. Then he asked if I would show him the gardens of the fairy castle.

I'd done worse in my time, I suppose, but I really didn't want to break my promise to Gallo. I shouldn't have worried – Ribbentrop just wanted to talk. He kept talking about how marvellous it would be to be together again in London, and in Paris too, when a few remaining problems had been resolved. He actually suggested a *partie carrée*, the two of us and Coco and her new beau.

We strolled deeper into the shrubbery and he told me that he'd done everything possible to keep us in Madrid. He'd ordered the German ambassador to put pressure on the Spaniards to refuse us an exit visa.[23] Franco was co-operative, but my husband lost his nerve and he ran. 'You are a pure and noble woman, a goddess,' he said. 'It cannot be possible for you to love a coward. Your husband is afraid of Churchill. I, on the other hand, fear no one.' I guess it was supposed to follow that I should love him instead of Lightning Brain. He was one of the very few men I knew I didn't like better than my husband.

At this point we were in a grove of trees, very private, and it made me think of Rhodes. Ribbentrop took a deep breath and he asked me, *he asked me*, if he could kiss me. I guess he was one Nazi who believed in negotiating.

He took another deep breath and began to talk some more. He went on and on and on about how long and how purely and truly he had loved me. I was something they had in Germany, the Eternal Feminine, which was all that was most desired and desirable in Creation embodied in one adorable object, or possibly subject, or possibly it was both a subject and an object. He lost me there. I thought he would never stop. Molotov must have agreed to split Poland with him to shut him up. Then he spoke for some time about Helen of Troy. He was hard to follow. He stopped for breath and I said, 'Yes,' with eyes downcast, all shy and girlish.

He squared his shoulders and reached out his arms, like a boy at dancing school who hadn't a clue how to hold a girl. He kissed me and he proved, as I guess he and his gang sincerely believed, that all men are not created equal. This was not news to me and he was nothing to write home about. I kissed him back and gave his lips just the tiniest flick with my tongue, like a serpent, like a snake. He began to tremble. He was shaking all over and clutching me, more to steady himself than to prolong the embrace. I forget the power I have. Some people look at me and see a scrawny woman who spends too much money on clothes and jewellery. Others think I'm hot stuff.

'I will leave you here, my Queen,' he said when he stopped quivering. 'I shall remember you in this garden until we meet again. Your image will have a holy shrine in my heart. I will not say *adieu*. I will say *Auf wiedersehen*, *au revoir*, until we meet again, *à bientôt, à la prochaine . . .*'

Gordie told me he returned to the terrace saying I'd asked for a few minutes alone to compose myself. The war and the partings it imposed on people who cared deeply for each other caused my sensitive nature almost unbearable pain.

'How did you and the Senhor know about the Countess Potocka?' I asked.

'An educated guess,' he said. 'There's always a Countess Potocka in play. Talleyrand had one.'[24]

'What happened finally with him and Napoleon? It ended badly, didn't it?'

'Not for Talleyrand. He died in his bed at a ripe old age after confessing all his sins, which took a long time. I'll lend you the book. You can read it on the voyage to the New World.'

Chapter Fifteen

We were interned in the Bahamas for the duration of the war. These are islands off the coast of Florida patrolled by the British and American navies, both of them working together. A German submarine was sighted in March 1942 and Government House, our residence, was surrounded with barbed wire at that time. A company of Cameron Highlanders, loyal Scotsmen naturally, were sent out, too, to protect us from 'kidnapping.'[1] But I knew from the first day that we were prisoners.

For a short time after London told us we had to leave Lisbon, I was hopeful. They promised to make Boysy a Governor General and I thought he'd go to replace the man who died that everyone liked so much. Canada's nothing special, but trains run to New York.

They sent us instead to Nassau in the Bahamas. The chief industry was tourism, the people mostly coloured, and there were labour troubles. The previous Governor made a hash of it and they sent him to Kampala, the capital of Uganda, which is worse, but this was the worst job in the British Empire in the Western Hemisphere.[2]

I gathered this from Gordie on the voyage out, but he explained it all more tactfully. He was coming with us to serve as *aide-de-camp* to the Governor General. He was a very nice boy and he reminded me of Freddy von und zu. He was thinner and wirier, with reddish hair and finer features, but they were both breezy and cheerful and pleasant to be with. It made me sad to think they might ever have to kill each other.

'No worries about me, Your Grace, I only stand and wait.' His two brothers, Alexander Andrew Montrose Wallingford-Just, called Sandy, and Louis William Archibald Raleigh Wallingford-Just, called Archie, were more likely to see action. Sandy was a great swot who knew Oriental languages, and he went, at some point, with some other chaps from the Black Watch to Burma.[3] Archie was a sportsman not a scholar, and he'd already fought in Norway. I think he ended up in Yugoslavia.

Gordie lent me Duff's book on Talleyrand. I didn't finish it, but parts of it were interesting. Talleyrand was ugly and irresistible to women and Duff seemed to like him. Gordie had some of Plum Wodehouse's books too and they were funny. There was a girl called Madeleine[4] who reminded me of Anne Lindbergh. Plum was rather mean about her. She said things like 'the stars are God's daisy chains' and 'morning glories are fairy trumpets.' Boysy continued with his 'shilling shockers,' as Gordie called them.

Our boat was actually diverted so we could be dropped off before it reached the American mainland. Boysy and I, as I suspected, would not be allowed to set foot on US soil until Roosevelt was safely re-elected. Nassau was more awful than I could have imagined. Government House was a nightmare. It was the most hideous house I had ever seen.[5] Even without a leaking roof and rodent droppings in the dining room, it would have been impossible. A Victorian horror. I refused to move in until it was completely renovated. I left my husband and Grey Philips, who had taken such an interest in our house in Paris, to supervise the work. Gordie took care of government business. He could sign Boysy's name as well as he could himself, and from time to time he brought him papers to see in manila folders that they called 'buff dockets.'

I had time on my hands and listened for hours to American radio programs. One of the first things I heard about was Anne Lindbergh's new book, *The Wave of the Future: A Confession of Faith*. This one was not about daisies or morning glories: it was about how the 'forces of the future' – and by that she meant the Nazis and others like them – would triumph over the 'forces of the past.' I ordered this book and I read it, not cover to cover the way I read Pearl Buck because Anne really didn't write as well as Pearl Buck and this book was so bad you could only read a little at a time. Fortunately, you didn't have to read every word to get the message: 'it is futile to get into a hopeless "crusade" to "save" civilisation.' 'There is no fighting the wave of the future any more than as a child you could fight against the gigantic roller that loomed up ahead of you suddenly.'[6]

The girl who used to lecture London dinner parties on the American Constitution was losing her mind. It was easy to see what the trouble was. Saint-Exupéry was back in the United States trying to rally support for the war, and he must still have been behaving himself. Anne was asking to be swept away. The poor child wanted to be ravished. It was a shame Saint-Exupéry hadn't overcome his scruples and taken her for the team.

On the other hand, the book was so hopeless and pathetic it gave Roosevelt a golden opportunity. He gave a radio address, which I heard, that made good use of it: 'There are men [everyone knew he was talking about poor Anne, but he was a Harvard man and a gentleman] who believe that . . . tyranny and slavery have become the surging wave of the future – and that freedom is an ebbing tide. But we Americans know that this is not true.'[7]

About that time, people realised that Hitler wasn't going to try to invade England, at least not that year, because it would be hard to do in fall weather and impossible in winter. Somebody in the German navy, and I don't envy him his job, had to explain to Hitler that high tide came at different times along the hundreds of miles of coast he was planning to invade, so his brilliant plan for a simultaneous assault would not work. Maybe those waves didn't want to be part of his future.

I didn't have much to do while I was waiting for our house to be ready and all I did do was follow the American election. Roosevelt seemed to have it pretty well in hand. Charles Lindbergh was 'above politics' and Anne was around the bend. Upper-class Republicans who'd been to Europe beat down the poorer, angrier ones who hadn't, so it wouldn't be the end of the world if their candidate won. Still, Gordie thought, it would be better and safer

Chapter Fifteen

with Roosevelt. The only wild card was held by that great moral and political leader Joseph P. Kennedy, the one who objected to tarts and libertines. The question was, would he, could he, split the Democrats? He'd stayed in London during the summer of 1940, reporting daily that Britain was near collapse. One of his, or the embassy's, code clerks was discovered to be keeping copies of top secret conversations between Roosevelt and Churchill.[8] I don't know if he was still interviewing beautiful refugees.

He skipped the party convention where Roosevelt was nominated for his third term, and he was due home in October, a month before the election. I thought a man who made him take off his pants in the White House was more than a match for him, but I was curious to see how Roosevelt would do it.

Kennedy was very rich. There were rumours he'd bought up a lot of radio time and the minute he set foot in the USA he'd rush to a studio and 'Tell the American people the truth.' That is to say, that the Brits were doomed and that the USA should make the best deal it could with Hitler while they still had some cards to play. It might be possible to pick up some of the British navy and parts of the Empire too. There were also rumours that the people Kennedy believed controlled the air waves did have some say in the matter and that they warned the President. I think maybe they did.

Roosevelt had squads of White House aides, and I don't know how many armed men – probably it just looked like an honour guard and a motorcycle escort – meet Kennedy in New York. He was allowed only a few minutes with the press and then he was whisked away to Washington, where the President urgently needed him. Mrs Kennedy was whisked away with him because people thought she had a calming influence. People said Roosevelt promised Kennedy he could be the first Catholic president in 1944 and that he'd support his son for Governor of Massachusetts. Kennedy was supposed to have said he had four sons and Roosevelt said, fine, he had forty-eight states. That may have been a joke, I'm not sure. I'm also not sure how long Roosevelt kept them in the White House. I imagine there were official meetings and a series of social events, lunch with Eleanor, dinner with, who knows, probably some of the State Department people Kennedy hated. Possibly even Sumner Welles. I hope Mr Welles was there for most of it. In the end, Kennedy agreed to go on the radio and support Roosevelt's re-election.[9] It reminded me of my husband after he abdicated. The United States is a free country, maybe freer than England, but certain kinds of men are not allowed to talk on the radio until other, better men know what they are going to say.

On Election Day, the machines in the big cities turned out the vote to re-elect the President. Gordie, who often lunched with us, said immigrant voters, first- and second-generation Americans, rallied in huge numbers. The Melting Pot voted in a big way for Roosevelt and for the fight they knew was coming, and new Americans of every nationality were enlisting in surprising numbers. The cities would have more firemen and postal clerks and street sweepers than they needed, he thought, but it wasn't true that democracy was disorganised and the Yanks didn't need secret police to get the job done.[10]

We moved into Government House, and Gordie was a godsend. Duff had sent him, so I felt I could be frank. I had to have my own bedroom. It was more than I could bear to be alone with Boysy in this ghastly house on this ghastly island not knowing what was happening in the war to, well, I was not completely frank, 'to all our friends,' is what I said. 'No worries,' he said, and he took care of it. He told my husband that he would have to wake him in the middle of the night with news bulletins that the War Cabinet would insist be brought to the immediate attention of the Governor General. Moreover, some of these top secret cables would be for his eyes only, so it might on the whole be more prudent as well as more considerate . . .

It took him some time to make the point, but one afternoon my husband, very sheepishly, suggested that I might wish to have my own room and that he would join me there whenever his duties permitted. His duties, I should say, consisted in playing golf and reading boys' true adventure stories. Gordie arranged events for him to attend to meet the locals and encourage them: pouring cement for the foundations of elementary schools and launching fishing boats to add protein to the diet of the poor, that sort of thing. 'Mostly bogus,' Gordie said. 'But much is in wartime.'

I had my duties too as the wife of the Governor General. I was *ex officio*, which means whether you want to or not, head of the Red Cross and the Daughters of the British Empire.[11] Gordie was a great help with this too. He volunteered to write to all the local ladies in my name. He said he helped his mother with her correspondence when it overwhelmed her, and I realised with a shock that his mother must be about my age. His letters asked dozens of local women for suggestions about ways to help the war effort, and he answered all of them, thanking them for their excellent ideas, some of which really were not bad. He wrote beautiful handwritten notes, and I couldn't have told you myself I hadn't written them, except I knew that I hadn't and I would never have been able to put things the way he did.

The local women got very involved and all I had to do was show up. They made Bundles for Britain – socks, magazines, shaving soap, and fruitcakes for soldiers; paperback books and writing paper and shaving soap and fruitcakes for POWs – and set up a clinic for babies. That was the best, really. It provided medical care and helpful advice for mothers. British ladies showed native women how to bathe and feed their babies, and a surprising lot of local women took advantage of it. Unmarried mothers were welcome too. They seemed grateful, poor things, and I didn't see that their babies were any worse than anybody else's.[12] The ladies did a lot for those less fortunate than themselves, and there were a lot less fortunate. Few tourists came in wartime, unemployment was increasing, and sometimes there were strikes and other demonstrations.

Gordie generally came to breakfast to brief my husband on the news of the day. It is much earlier, or later, in the Bahamas than it is in Europe, that is, lots of things had already happened by the time he got there to tell us about them. Then he'd drive me to my first engagement. Sometimes he came with a driver and we chatted in the back of the car. Sometimes he came without a driver and told me things about the war that Lightning Brain wasn't allowed to hear. Nobody trusted him, and the Governor General heard exactly nothing except whatever I was supposed to pass on to Ribbentrop through Coco Chanel. Gordie and I got chummy and he told me about his fiancée, 'the best girl in the world.' Mary was good at math, or at 'maths' as he said, and her war job was very hush-hush, but she wasn't a swot. She loved the outdoors. I asked to see her picture. She was a nice-looking girl, not a goddess like Diana Cooper or Edwina Mountbatten, but pretty in a down-to-earth sort of way. She had bright, intelligent eyes and she looked lively.

Gordie went to church and he thought we should go ourselves to set an example. People were suffering great privations and many, too many, had gotten or would soon get news that would break their hearts. The Church of England with its prayer book and its Bible could bring solace, he said, through the beauty of its language even to people who didn't believe a word of it was literally true. Personally, he said, he thought a lot of it was true, if you thought about it the right way. In any case, it was a national treasure and the Governor General ought to support it.

The Bible, it turned out, was the sticking point for my husband. He positively refused to go to church because he was afraid they'd make him read bits of the Bible aloud and he couldn't pronounce the names of the people or the places. Gordie had an excellent suggestion: the honour should be offered to people he described as 'community leaders'. He proposed a man he knew, one Abe Beresford-Jones, who led a troop of Boy Scouts, a postmaster with a strong sense of civic responsibility. 'He's an imposing fellow,' Gordie said, 'with enormous dignity and presence. He looks like

Prester John.' This meant nothing to me or to Lightning Brain, but as we soon discovered, it was the title of a book by the man who had been Governor General of Canada. A book that takes place in Africa.

The vicar agreed to ask Mr Beresford-Jones to read the lesson, which is what they called it, on the next Sunday, and I thought he read it very nicely. He had a deep voice and you could hear it during the hymns. Splendid *basso profundo*, Gordie whispered to me during 'Onward, Christian Soldiers.' Beresford-Jones was very tall, very handsome, and very black, just like the man in the book, as it turned out. The Governor General who had not read the book was whiter than usual, white with rage, and as we drove back to Government House after the service he shouted at Gordie in language I never imagined he knew and which would have disappointed the Dowager Queen and Empress, his mother, very much. Not as much as his marriage, maybe, but very much. 'You have betrayed me, you effing cad. You are worse than that effing blighter Ribbentrop. This is a million times worse than his beastly deal with the effing Reds because you have made an effing fool of me. I will never get out of this effing hellhole now it looks like I've gone effing native, you effing cur.' He was screaming at the top of his lungs, and we were driving in an open car so everyone could see we went to church.

Gordie took it all very well. He thought he'd mentioned the man's striking appearance and his resemblance to Prester John, so clearly his ancestry was not European. He had assumed His Royal Highness the Governor General was acquainted with the book because of his taste for the genre.

'Genre? What are you talking about? How dare you?' Boysy said. We were riding, as I said, in an open car and I managed to persuade him to wait until we got home to continue the conversation.

He was calmer after a glass or two of sherry, and willing to listen when Gordie predicted things would look up, and they did, but not right away. Beresford-Jones had such an extremely nice voice that the vicar asked him if he would join the choir, and his fame spread and before long the tourist trade improved. People from Florida began to vacation in the Bahamas, more women than men. Of course it was wartime, so women had time on their hands. Women began coming in droves and they went to church on Sunday morning, although very few of them seemed to be familiar with the Anglican service. Some were heard comparing Mr Beresford-Jones to Paul Robeson, who was a celebrated American actor and singer and Communist.

My husband was beside himself. He'd gotten a copy of the Prester John book, and with that and all the talk about Paul Robeson, he convinced himself that Beresford-Jones was going to lead a native insurrection bank-rolled by Miami Jews.

I was present when he accused Gordie of plotting this. 'Sir, that is risible.'

Fortunately, Boysy did not understand and that gave Gordie time to collect himself.

'I would suggest, sir, that one might see it differently. I believe he's a natural leader of men and that if we let him organise government employees, beginning with the post office, we could negotiate with them a modest improvement in working conditions. We can't raise their wages in wartime, but there are things we could do to make their lives more agreeable. It could be a model for other employers.'

The Governor General of the Bahamas would not let this scheme go forward until he could meet Beresford-Jones and take his measure. He read men, not books.

I must say, the fellow behaved very well when he met my husband. 'How do you do, Your Royal Highness?' And without talking too long, he thanked him for all he had done for the Bahamas and for his kind letter which he'd always treasure.

'What's your name?' Rather abrupt.

'Beresford-Jones, Your Royal Highness.' Boysy was supposed to have written him a letter, so it was an odd question.

Chapter Fifteen

'Your Christian name. Abe, is it? Named for Abraham Lincoln, or Lin-Cohen as some might say. I suppose you want to free the slaves here, eh?'

'Why, no, sir. Slavery was abolished in the British Empire before the reign of Queen Victoria.'

'But you are named for Lincoln, eh?'

'No, sir. My given name is Abimelech.'

'That's a Christian name?'

Honest Abe replied it was Biblical, from the Old Testament.

'Jewish?'

'No, sir.' He was growing more and more uncomfortable, and Gordie told me he must have been embarrassed because Abimelech, you might not know, was a king who, unlike King David, did not sleep with another man's wife, at least he didn't on the only chance he had that is mentioned in the Bible.[13]

Gordie tried to change the subject to the Boy Scouts, but Boysy persisted. 'You have Jewish friends?'

'Yes, sir, I do. Many of the merchants have been most generous with the Boy Scout food drives.'

'Are you, my good man, by any chance a Freemason?'

Beresford-Jones smiled and almost laughed. 'No, sir, of course not. The lodges in the Bahamas are lily-white.'

'But you know men who are Freemasons?'

'Some of my best friends, sir. A couple of them want to nominate me to break the colour bar.'

My husband ordered Gordie to put him under surveillance and Gordie did spend a lot of time with him. Their acquaintance turned out to be a great help. The native population was restless and Gordie feared that enemy agents might be working among them. He suggested we do what the French were doing in Africa, translate all the awful things Hitler said about Negroes in *Mein Kampf* and circulate them widely. Boysy thought it was a stupid idea and refused to approve it, so Beresford-Jones got the book out of a public library – this was British soil, after all, and they don't ban books –

and he reprinted certain passages and had his Boy Scouts put them in every mailbox in certain neighbourhoods.

We were allowed to visit the United States in the fall of 1941. We stayed with the British ambassador, Lord Halifax, and that was a little awkward because my husband was still cross he wasn't made ambassador to Washington after the previous one died, and also, Lord Halifax remarked to somebody that he thought my hands and fingers were 'very common.'[14] Well, I was aware of that and wore gloves whenever I could. I thought it very unfair under the circumstances, because I hadn't seen Marie-Ange since the spring of 1940 and Nassau was extremely primitive. Things really never got very matey between Roosevelt and my husband or between Eleanor and myself, but they gave us a nice lunch in the White House, without a hot dog in sight, and they were nice enough to invite Katherine and Herman Rogers too.[15] It seems that FDR and Herman were great pals and they had all known each other for ages. Pearl Harbor was attacked a few weeks later and the Americans were in. Hitler had attacked Russia in June, so people felt they had a fighting chance to beat him.

We were invited back to Washington in the spring of 1943. On the very day that we had luncheon at the White House, with Herman and Katherine Rogers invited again, we got word during the dinner Lord Halifax was giving for us that serious rioting had broken out in Nassau.[16] FDR said he'd send the Marines. Eleanor was appalled to hear he'd dispatch Americans to shoot strikers – coloured strikers – and he promised they'd do nothing of the kind. They'd prevent looting and direct traffic and in a week or two 'our good friend' – he meant Lightning Brain –'can return and set things right. I can see he has his finger on the pulse of the Bahamas.'

By the time Boysy returned, the Marines, and Gordie and Abe Beresford-Jones, had matters well in hand. My husband had an entirely new opinion of Roosevelt and he said at every opportunity that Franklin knew he had his finger on the pulse of the Bahamas.

The Atlantic shipping lanes were safe with him on guard in Nassau, and those in the know knew how important he really was.

The islands became peaceful. Wounded soldiers were sent there to convalesce and I visited them. Cookie got a lot of good publicity from doing it, so I thought I might as well do it too, and Gordie kept cooking up bogus events for my husband to preside over. There were a couple of unsolved murders while we were there, one involving people we knew quite well. Boysy got mixed up with a sleazy Swede, Axel Wenner-Green, who knew Göring and Charles Bedaux. He was a suspicious character who followed Sumner Welles around when he was in Europe during the phony war; and he was certainly up to no good in South America until the Americans blacklisted him.[17] Lightning Brain was always a sucker for rich men who said they cared only about peace. He was awfully cut up about the death of his brother, the Duke of Kent, training to be a pilot, in the summer of 1943. But all in all, things were pretty quiet.

Chapter Sixteen

My chief concern during those years was, as it had always been, my wardrobe. I continued to buy clothes from Coco Chanel and I told her exactly what I wanted. This was the way I communicated with Ribbentrop. The British government, as I may have mentioned, didn't trust my husband and they told him nothing about the fighting except what they wanted me to pass on to my devoted admirer. More often, Gordie gave me the information I was supposed to send. He worked the code too, and it was complicated. Words were used, dressmaking terms to which other meanings could be given, but mostly we relied on measurements. The number and placement of beads and *paillettes* and covered buttons translated into longitude and latitude and dates and times. Coco had a complete set of my measurements and a dressmaker's dummy exactly like me. A dummy cannot take the place of live fittings, needless to say – one has to see how the dress moves when you walk or sit – but it was fine as a base for calculations.

I couldn't have done it myself, but as time went on I got the hang of it. Many times I was used to send wrong information, 'disinformation', Gordie called it, 'strategic deception'. Most of what I sent Coco in the first years of the war was misleading, not very wrong but wrong enough. If information is too far off the mark, the people getting it stop trusting you. Gordie began to tell me what was bogus and what wasn't, and I felt he trusted me more than he trusted my husband. Or maybe, at first, he was testing me.

The British got the Italians out of East Africa in no time, before Pearl Harbor, and Gaston Palewski helped liberate Djibouti. Gordie told me that the Italian Foreign Minister was believed to have asked to rejoin his squadron and been ordered to remain in Rome.

Once the Americans were in, they joined in on the landings in French North Africa. This was when we first heard about General Eisenhower. I thought his name sounded German, but I guess the Melting Pot did all that people hoped it would. I ordered a lot of new clothes in the months before the Allies went into Morocco and Algeria.

The radio operators had standing orders to transmit immediately and exactly as written anything the Duchess wanted sent to the House of Chanel. Strict secrecy was imposed because it would be bad for morale, disastrous, if people knew that the Duchess cared about fashion in the middle of a world war. There would be more riots if the public, making all kinds of sacrifices with everything rationed, including fabric, knew how much money I was spending. I imagine a lot of people had to be bribed to make this work, but I also think the bills were used to request information. The sums were staggering. The radio operators despised me, and it's a tribute to British discipline that not a word of this got out, as I am pretty sure it didn't.

I had little to do or think about, and I was very blue. Gordie took me to church sometimes. He thought that singing hymns might cheer me up and that the beautiful language of the prayer book could not fail to raise my spirits. 'My mother finds it a great comfort,' he said. Church, however, did nothing for me, but I began to take an interest in the war and to puzzle out the codes. With every new campaign I got to order a lot of lovely dresses, and they all arrived at Government House, generally routed through Switzerland. If I didn't get my new clothes, people might suspect my messages were bogus.

The African campaigns went well, and people began to talk cheerfully about invading Europe. Gordie told me that Roosevelt and Churchill met in Casablanca and General de Gaulle forced himself into the meeting by sheer gall, you might say, and plans were being made to invade Italy.

'Where?' I asked.

'Ah,' Gordie said. 'That's a secret and they haven't told me.' This was very early in 1943, before we went to Washington.

I was, as you may imagine, wild to know this, and I learned more during the spring after we got home. It was really too good a story not to tell, and by now I was certain Gordie trusted me. The British and the Americans, and, he said, Canadians too, were all going to land in Sicily and then cross the Bay of Naples. 'A straight shot to Rome,' he said. 'And there's a hope, more than a hope we think, that the Italians will overthrow Mussolini before we get there. The Duce may have got wind of it. He's reshuffled his Cabinet and taken over the Foreign Ministry himself and made Count Ciano ambassador to the Vatican.'[1]

I remember Lisbon. 'I thought we were not so keen on this Pope.'

'He must know the tide's turning. The Count should be safe as houses.' There were to be smaller landings, 'feints' he said, in other places, among the Greek islands and in Sardinia, and it was no secret that de Gaulle wanted to land in Corsica and cross there so that French troops could descend on Rome from the north.

That is what Gordie told me, and I don't think he knew the whole story then himself. There were no 'feints' in fact, but the biggest disinformation campaign of the war up to that point was carried out to make the Germans believe that the Allies would land in Sardinia and at several places in the eastern Mediterranean. A body, dressed as a British officer carrying invasion plans, was put into the sea off the coast of Spain.[2] Churchill was supposed to be going mad and trying to avenge some terrible tragedy in the First War. If you spent a lot of time with Hitler, you might expect leaders to lose their marbles every now and then. I took a great interest in this, and Gordie showed me maps and taught me how to read them. He asked me if I'd like a wireless, and I said I would. I was now more grateful than ever to him that I had my own bedroom. I would have lost my mind if I had had to sleep in the same bed as Boysy that spring.

One afternoon, we were placing an order for my summer

wardrobe. I put a lot of thought into it. I actually imagined I'd be wearing these dresses in Rome, possibly even in Capri, which everyone said was so beautiful. Pretty, feminine dresses, light silks and painted chiffon, with not so many buttons, hardly any buttons at all. I was thinking of sashes that could be tied and untied in the twinkling of an eye. Gordie was working out some coordinates with flower *appliqués*. 'Daisies,' I said, 'and roses. And maybe a bunch of silk roses, beach roses, not cabbage roses, at the waist to fasten onto the sash.'

'No,' he said. 'Beach roses go on the left shoulder, five centimetres from the shoulder seam.'

I was looking at an ordnance map. 'No, that's wrong. That's Sicily. I make it there, a little place called Gela on the south coast.'

'Jolly good. You've got the hang of it. You can do this yourself now, if you like. You don't need me any more.'

'But you, I mean we, *are* landing in Sicily,' I said. Gordie couldn't be a traitor any more than he could be a pineapple. He was the truest, squarest Brit you could meet.

'That's right.'

'Then why are we telling that to Coco to tell her friend to tell Ribbentrop?'

'There's a reason. You must trust me, ma'am.'

'Never mind, ma'am.' I'm just a simple *demi-mondaine*. I will not do this, Gordie. I won't, and you can't make me.' I realised the minute I said it that it was a stupid thing to say. They didn't need me. Gordie handed in my orders in sealed envelopes. He could send any message he wanted. Gordie could write letters to Coco or to Ribbentrop in my name and no one would be the wiser.

'I can tell you this much, ma'am. A decision has been made to boost Ribbentrop's stock. It's come to be known that Göring doesn't trust you.' I could have told them that years ago. 'He believes you are toying with Ribbentrop, and that he is a credulous, love-blinded fool.' Göring was in some ways the worst of them, but he was not the stupidest, or so I thought.

'Yes,' I said. Gordie was telling the truth, no doubt about it. So far, so good.

'So, this time, Ribbentrop will be right and his stock will rise with the Führer. And that will be useful in years to come.'

'And this invasion will fail and you, we, will not have a straight shot to Rome.'

'No,' Gordie said. 'It's not like that at all. The Jerries have taken the bait. They're reinforcing Sardinia and they've moved several divisions into Greece and Yugoslavia. They think Italy's a sideshow anyway. They always have.'

That certainly rang true.

'Please trust me, Your Grace. This is just a little crumb to toss to Ribbentrop, so he can say "I told you so", and so next time they'll listen to him.'

I don't think the boy was lying to me, and if he was, I couldn't stop him from sending the message.

The Allies landed in Sicily in July and Mussolini was deposed even before they crossed to the mainland. Gallo voted with the majority of some inner circle to remove him and begin peace talks with the Allies.[3] It was all going according to plan, and then it stopped going according to plan. Mussolini was arrested and imprisoned, but the Germans rescued him and put him back in power. The Allies made no progress towards Rome. The Germans were dug in south of the city and the fighting was terrible, with heavy casualties.

I kept my radio on all night, and as summer became fall and fall winter, or as much of a winter as we got in the Bahamas, I got used to not knowing what was really happening. I listened to the BBC, but the news sounded the same every day and every night. Things happened in Europe and, as I said, we heard about them long after they actually happened even if the news was not delayed by wartime censorship. You feel there's nothing you can do, even if you couldn't have done anything anyway, when it's over when you hear about it, and I almost stopped listening.

I went about my 'duties,' the stupid round of volunteer work that I never would have done except the Governor General's wife had to, and the only pleasant parts of my day were my chats with Gordie, who told me, whenever he could, more than the BBC. One day, looking troubled, he said they'd heard that the Pope had refused to give sanctuary in the Vatican to Count and Countess Ciano and their three little children and that they might be in Germany.[4] Nobody knew how that had happened or on what terms they went or if Mussolini had agreed to it or if he'd been asked. Gallo in the hands of the Germans. 'God help him,' I said.

'May God protect us all, Your Grace.' I knew things were bad when he called me that.

Christmas came and went. Cartier was not exporting in those years, or not to us. People got drunk and jolly on New Year's and predicted that 1944 would be the year when Hitler got what was coming to him. The Daughters of the British Empire asked if they could burn a yule log at Government House on Twelfth Night, and I let them. A blazing fire isn't so pleasant on a tropical or semi-tropical island as it is on a snowy night, but I didn't mind.

One morning shortly after the yule log had burned itself out, I woke up early. I wasn't sleeping well. The sky was grey. We were close to the equator and that was why, Gordie had explained, the days didn't seem as long or as short as they did in England. There was no need to get up. Gordie generally came for me at about ten. I preferred to have breakfast on a tray in my room, but from time to time I got dressed and went down to have breakfast with my husband. If I didn't see him then, I generally saw him at lunch, when he would tell me bits of news that irritated him. Few things about the war or the conduct of the war pleased him, and his disposition soured in the Bahamas. There wasn't much to do there.

I was lying in bed, wondering if I ought to make the effort to dress for breakfast or laze under the covers for a while, when I heard it. Gordie had gotten me the best wireless to be had. Even so, there was a lot of static, signals were jammed, weather affected it. But there was no mistaking this bulletin. I heard it clearly.

It was announced in Rome and a few hours later in Berlin: the execution of five traitors by Italian authorities in the northern city of Verona. All were members of the Fascist Grand Council who had voted, in July of last year, to remove Mussolini from power. The most prominent was Count Galeazzo Ciano, Mussolini's son-in-law, who had served as Foreign Minister from 1936 until he was removed and made ambassador to the Vatican in February of 1943. They read the names of the four other men, but I did not hear them.[5]

I got up and got dressed and went to sit outdoors, on the chair beneath the portico of Government House, where I liked to wait in the morning for Gordie to pick me up. My husband didn't miss me at breakfast and my maid, seeing my bed empty, didn't bother about a breakfast tray. I was able to be alone for a couple of hours and I don't remember thinking of a single thing.

Gordie came earlier than he usually did, without a driver. 'Good morning, Your Grace.' He knew and he must have known that I knew.

'Good morning, Gordie.'

'Is there anything I can do for you?'

I didn't answer him and he tried again.

'You've been working hard with all your charities. I thought you might like a day off. I brought some sandwiches and a bottle of wine. I could take you for a picnic, or a sail.'

I looked into the car. There was a picnic hamper on the back seat and a blanket. I believe that nice boy would have tried to comfort me in any way I wanted, but I didn't want anyone even to touch me. 'Take me to the clinic.' I spent the morning watching English ladies washing little black babies for an hour or two, and I thought about Marie-Ange and little Charles de Gaulle Amadou.

Usually I went home to lunch and had a rest and changed my clothes for whatever I had to do in the afternoon. That day I had a full schedule, a luncheon and an afternoon session with the Red Cross and a banquet honouring the woman who had made up the most Bundles for Britain, at which I was called on to make a toast. I cannot remember a word I said or what I was wearing. People told me afterwards that my toast was extremely moving and that my gesture of appearing – me always on the top of the list of the world's best-dressed women – at a formal dinner in my Red Cross uniform was an inspiration to all the girls and women of the Empire.

I was tired when I got home and I went directly upstairs. On the table by my bed I found the Anglican *Book of Common Prayer*. Gordie must have left it there. Those prayer books have a ribbon to mark the place, instead of a bookmark that might fall out, and it opened towards the back of the book, to Psalm 57.[6]

> Be merciful unto me, O God, be merciful unto me, for my soul trusteth in thee:
> And under the shadow of thy wings shall be my refuge, until this tyranny be over-past.

Chapter Seventeen

The Allies were no closer to Rome then, early in 1944, than they had been in July when, obviously, they'd been expected to show up any minute. Gordie, to his credit, never tried to tell me it didn't matter that I'd given Ribbentrop the actual plans. He stayed as close to me as he decently could for the next several weeks, joining us for dinner almost every night. It would have been difficult for me to dine tête-à-tête with my husband because I found it almost impossible to make conversation. I used to find it easy to jolly him along, agreeing with all the imbecile things he said. Now I felt that if I opened my mouth, I would scream.

In February, Charles Bedaux was arrested in North Africa and flown to Miami, where he killed himself before he could be brought to trial.[1] I have no idea what he was doing or if my husband knew what he was doing, but Boysy complained a great deal about being left out of things. Look what a hash they were making of Italy. He felt sure he could do better, and he thought people kept him on this wretched little island because they were jealous of his abilities.

Then things began to go better in Italy. The Allies landed closer to Rome,[2] north of where the Germans were dug in, and the Italians were hiding Allied prisoners who escaped and fighting the Germans themselves. Partisan groups were active, Gordie said, in the north, and there were terrible reprisals when they attacked German forces successfully.

He said we must get to work again on an order to send to Mme Chanel. This was going to be the big push into France, and there was lots and lots of disinformation already in the works – a huge campaign, agents who'd been turned, and whole networks of purely imaginary agents supposedly reporting to real agents, who collected their pay and filed their expense statements, which had more truth in them than their reports. There were dummy airfields too, and masses of tanks and landing craft, all bogus but looking real enough in photos taken from a plane. 'Strategic deception' on a scale larger than it had ever been practised was going to be needed, because the Germans knew the Allies were going to invade France from England and the coast is what it is, all in plain view, with not a lot of places to choose from. Of course, efforts were made to suggest that they thought the quickest way to Berlin was through Norway, but nobody expected even Ribbentrop to believe that.

After a lot of very smart people thought of everything over a period of years, including, I suppose, making sure I never lost my temper with Ribbentrop, it boiled down to this: the Allies were going to land in Normandy, which is not the obvious place. The Channel is wider there than it is anywhere else unless you are practically in Spain, and farms are separated by funny little hedges that make it hard to move cross-country. The shortest crossing, where England and France are separated only by the Straits of Dover, is between Dover and the Pas de Calais. A *pas* is a step, like in a *faux pas*. The Pas de Calais is not only closer to England than Normandy, it is closer to Germany and on the other side of a lot of French rivers that you have to cross to get to Germany. It was closer, too, to the places where the Germans were launching their rockets. It was the obvious place, and that is where the Germans had to expect the Allies to land.[3]

I didn't have the heart to order any new clothes. I was sick of the game. I didn't want new clothes. I wanted all of them dead – Hitler, Göring, Himmler, Ribbentrop, and Mussolini. Most of all, I wanted Il Duce dead. Details had come out about Gallo's execution. In Italy, traitors aren't just shot, they are shot in the back. You would think it wouldn't be hard to kill somebody that way, but the firing squad hadn't managed to do it. Somebody had to fire a shot, not just once but twice, into his forehead. Point-blank, as he lay on the ground.[4] I read this in the newspaper.

We had a lot of soldiers recovering from bullet wounds in Nassau and I asked the nurses about the pain they'd suffered. They said people went into shock right away when they were shot and so they didn't feel any pain at all. I felt I shouldn't ask the men and I didn't believe the nurses, who, after all, had never been shot themselves. So, as I always did, I asked Gordie. He was chewing a pencil and looking at a map of France, and he replied that his brother Archie'd been shot in Norway and he said it hurt like hell. He realised his mistake immediately. 'Archie's brave as a lion, but he does like to be fussed over. Mother said he made more of a broken leg than most chaps would of an amputation.'

I didn't say anything and the silence got awkward.

'The missionary Livingstone wrote an account of being bitten by a lion, ma'am. It was frightening, but he didn't feel a thing once the beast's jaws closed on his shoulder. He offers it as proof of God's mercy.'

'That's nice,' I said. That's the Brits all over. They're being eaten by a lion and they think God's helping them keep a stiff upper lip. Livingstone must have lived to tell about it, though, so maybe it's a true story.

'It can only have been a matter of minutes, Your Grace. He can't have suffered long. I cannot tell you how sorry I am.'

'I am sick of this, Gordie. I am sick of playing with them. I want to write to Ribbentrop in plain language.' I hoped the Nazis would shoot him themselves when they found out what a fool he was, and I hoped they'd have to do it many times over many days.

Gordie thought for a minute. 'Brilliant.'

The operators had orders to send the messages exactly as they were written, not to change a letter or a number. Gordie always handed them in for me and he told me they made wry faces but never said a word, at least not in his presence.

Chapter Seventeen

I snatched up a pad of writing paper and wrote this:

DARLING – This may sound callous [underlined], but I am desperately bored and lonely on this horrid little island. I long to step out with you in the *partie carrée* you promised me when last we met, too long ago, my true knight.

And then I said it again, so he could not possibly misunderstand

Others may think me callous (underlined again) but you know now, my love, or I hope you do, that I would step over any body (keep the words separate) to return to your embrace.

Gordie was horrified. 'Your Grace, you cannot send this. It's monstrous. What would people think?'

'My good name? No worries, dear boy.'

'It's not subtle, if I may say so. Or credible. Nobody could be so selfish and heartless. What's this about a *partie carrée?*'

'He suggested it in Lisbon, us and Coco and her new friend, his old friend. We were alone when he said it, so it has to come from me.'

'Your Grace, this wouldn't be credible in a shilling shocker coming from the depraved mistress of the leader of the gang. Any fool could see it's bogus.'

'Ribbentrop won't think it's bogus. And I'm not finished.' I added seventeen kisses, little Xs in three groups of five, plus two. 'Have them send it like that, so it's easy to keep track, three groups of five, followed by two more.'

'It's a good idea to write to him directly, I agree, but this, forgive me, it's ridiculous.'

'So is Ribbentrop. Not subtle, ridiculous. You've met him, but you don't know him and I do.'

I don't claim credit for the success of the Normandy landings. I was never ambitious in that way, but they were a success. My husband and I were having breakfast together on D-Day. Things have already happened, as I said, when the sun rises in Nassau, and the beachhead had been established. The Duke didn't like to have a radio in a room where meals were eaten, but I'd heard the news already, and the King's speech too, which I thought was rather good.

My husband was reading the newspaper when I took my place across from him. It was a special edition of a Miami paper with headlines that took up half the front page. 'They've landed at Normandy,' he said. 'Odd, isn't it? Must be some crazy idea of that madman de Gaulle, always seeking to thrust himself forward. Much better to have crossed the Straits of Dover. I can't imagine why they didn't.'

Gordie came in, flushed and happy, with some buff dockets. 'Very good morning to you both, Your Royal Highness, Your Grace. This is it. The Germans were completely surprised and they still haven't reacted.'

'The BBC says it's the big push,' my husband said. 'But a lot of things are bogus in wartime. There may yet be an attack on the Pas de Calais.'

'You may be right, sir. The bulk of the German infantry is still east of the Seine. They aren't moving their troops, so they must think so.'

'Won't you join us, Gordie?' I felt I'd be less likely to lose my temper if he stayed.

My husband continued to read the newspaper, rather rudely, I thought, because he wasn't ever a great reader, as I may have mentioned, but today he seemed intent on reading the entire *Miami Herald.*

'Rome's fallen,' he said, 'two days ago. Lost in all the excitement about France.'

'Rome was liberated, sir,' Gordie said. 'That's the word from Whitehall.'

'No matter,' my husband said. 'If they do get to Paris, darling,

Chapter Seventeen

you'll have far less bother about your new frocks. That should be a weight off your mind.'

The war wrapped up. It took almost another year, but the end was never in question. It took less than three months to get from the coast of Normandy to Paris, after it took nearly a year to get from Naples to Rome. People began to talk about when they knew it was really over – the writing was on the wall after Pearl Harbor, some said, certainly after Stalingrad, many thought – before it was really over.

New Year's Eve was celebrated as it hadn't been for years. 1945, people said, was sure to be the year that Hitler got what was coming to him. Abe Beresford-Jones got what was coming to him: a knighthood in the New Year's Honours List, for his services in furthering the prosperity of the Bahamas and in fostering co-operation and understanding among its citizens. Boysy gave the toast to Sir Abimelech. Gordie wrote it and it was very nice, about the brotherhood of man and the coming triumph of democracy. Abe replied modestly about everyone doing his bit, and we all sang 'For He's a Jolly Good Fellow'. My husband was more pleased than I thought he would be, and as we were being driven home from the party he said that he'd always had his finger on the pulse of the Bahamas, and now that he'd whipped the Western Hemisphere into shape, they might make him Viceroy of India. I'd have jumped at that once, but now the idea left me cold. I'd been feeling cold for a long time.

The war continued to go well and one morning in April, Gordie showed up quite early again while we were at breakfast. He was bursting with some news. 'Mussolini's dead, ma'am, sir. The Italians have killed him themselves.'

'Oh, thank God,' I said. 'Really? You're certain?'

He took a buff docket out of his briefcase. 'Pictures taken by our forces in Milan, sir.'

Usually Gordie did all his work for him, and the dockets he actually brought to him at breakfast, before he went to his office, were so important that he could not appear in public, so to speak, without knowing about them.

'You should have a look at these photographs, sir. Rather brutal, I'm afraid,' he said, handing the file to my husband. 'They strung him up with Signora Petacci. It all happened before our forces got there. We could not have countenanced it, of course.' There was the faintest twitch at the corner of his mouth and I believe to this day the British gave them all the time they needed. 'Even after we got there, it took some time, quite some time, before the crowd would let us cut them down.'

'Shocking. Revolting.' Boysy looked at a series of photographs. 'Savages.'

'Those injuries were inflicted *post mortem*, sir. You see there's no clotting.'

'The Germans would never do this sort of thing to Hitler.'

'Rather not, sir,' Gordie said.

'Show real depravity.'

'The events can be seen in another way, sir. There is something to be said for rough justice. Troubles the sleep of tyrants, as they say.'

'They're not really Romans.'

'This is Milan, sir.'

'Modern Italians, I mean, they don't descend from the Romans. They're mongrels, a mixture of Central Asian tribes and Africans and lots of Jews in all the large cities.'

'Vikings in Sicily,' Gordie added.

'I want to see the pictures,' I said.

'I forbid it,' my husband said. This was a first. 'They're not fit to be seen by a lady, not fit to be seen by a woman of any description.'

'I want them.'

'It's popular vengeance in the traditional manner, ma'am. Honestly, I think you'd better not.'

I drew myself very erect in my chair and tried to be as British as I could be. 'Leff-tenant Wallingford-Just, the photographs, please, at once.'

'Your Grace,' he said, taking the folder from my husband and handing it to me.

The pictures were black-and-white, and surprisingly clear. I looked at them for a long time. My heart began beating wildly.

Chapter Eighteen

Days after the Italians dealt with Mussolini, the Russians reached Berlin. Hitler and some of his inner circle killed themselves and the Allies were making plans to put the rest on trial. This was what the future held for both Göring and Ribbentrop. The Japanese were defeated too and the war was over and in the summer of 1946 we were able to return to La Croë, where we hadn't been since I was packing and listening to planes flying off to bomb Genoa. The Riviera has never been the same for me since.

Duff Cooper was back too as ambassador to France, and I asked him about the trials. He said they'd begin as soon as they could get the French and Russians to agree on the presumption of innocence. I thought he was joking, but he wasn't. 'Being British, you'll make sure they all have lawyers. I hope you won't give them anyone good. Like Norman Birkett.'

'Not to worry, my dear,' he said. 'Funny you should say it. He's going to be one of the British judges,[1] assuming we can iron out a few details with our friends.'

I got a cold feeling in my stomach. 'You planned it all, didn't you, from the start – our cruise and my divorce, and all the rest, everything?'

'My dear, I'm only a flea on the axle of History's chariot, amazed by all the dust I can raise.'

'Who said that?'

'Aesop and Sir Francis Bacon and a friend of mine.'[2]

'You know what I mean.' He did. 'Ribbentrop started sending me flowers in 1935 and the first thing you asked me after I said I'd help was if I knew the Count.' People thought we had an affair in China. Edda was supposed to think so herself even though I left more than a year before he first arrived and never went back. I guess she wasn't the sort of girl who did her homework either.

'We wanted to keep Italy neutral,' Duff said. 'We thought he wanted that too. Sumner Welles was certain of it.'[3]

I didn't say a word. I just stared back at him.

'When one plan fails, one tries another. We needed many arrows in our quiver.'

'Right, and it was fine with you, it was swell, that it took a year to get to Rome. Every German soldier in Italy was one less in Russia or France.'

'Oh, my dear, *c'est la guerre.*' He stopped to weigh his words. 'I never imagined you'd grow so fond of each other.' He was a kind man and 'of each other' was a kind thing to say. 'The Count was thought to be fickle.'

Fickle! The Brits didn't make Duff an ambassador for nothing. He didn't have to say it, but people thought the Duchess of Windsor was fickle too. She didn't always leave the dance with the boy who brought her.

Duff went on. 'He was intelligent and resourceful. I honestly thought he had a good chance to come out of it with a whole skin. But for his children, he might have escaped abroad. Others did.'[4]

'What will happen if, by any chance, Ribbentrop and Göring are found guilty?'

'They will be hanged.'

'That's not enough.'

'I know,' Duff said, and he looked very grim. 'We are civilised people.'

The trials began and Ribbentrop, who must have been obsessed, claimed that he'd been an honourable statesman working tirelessly for peace, thwarted by that Machiavellian fiend Ciano. The evidence against him must be dismissed because Count Ciano kept two diaries, one to publish if the Axis lost and another if they won.[5]

It was news to me that he'd kept a diary at all. Gordie came to visit while his fiancée was having her wedding dress fitted in Paris. Worth was doing it. They'd done her mother's and her grandmother's. I asked him what he knew, and he knew a lot. Gallo's wife – and it came out that this was her nickname for him – was loyal to him in the end, not to her father, and she smuggled his diary into Switzerland. People said the Germans sent a girl to get it for them – Gordie blushed as he told me this – but if there was such a person, and who could be sure of anything in wartime, more likely than not she'd helped the Countess. A young Italian nobleman was involved too, some said the Countess's lover, but both of them risked their lives to preserve her husband's memory.[6]

'I suppose it's all very hush-hush, except for what they're using at the trials.'

'Rather. Under lock and key with the Yalies, I'm afraid.'

'Have you read it?'

'I've seen the bits Ribbentrop claims are false. The Count tried to keep them from invading Poland, and Hitler laughed at him. He was incapable of understanding German policy because he was a "man of the South".'[7]

To think Gallo had to listen to things like that. He was very proud and sensitive, really. 'I wish the Russians had got him alive. Hitler, I mean.'

'So do I, Your Grace. Lots of us do.'

Willie Maugham was back at Cap Ferrat and I'd asked him to spend the weekend with us so Gordie could meet him. He always had his nose in a book and sure enough, before long, they were thick as thieves. I went for a walk in the garden on Sunday morning. I didn't like so much to look at the sea, and I could hear them talking through the open doors of the breakfast room. You can learn a lot by eavesdropping on Somerset Maugham.

'She knows about the diary, sir,' Gordie was saying. 'I told her everyone assumes he wrote it knowing that Mussolini could demand to see it at any time. There was nothing personal except about his father and his children, and no mention of any woman except his wife. And I tried to downplay the part about Fräulein Burckhardt.'

'That is the most fantastic part,' Maugham said. 'Sending Burck-hardt's granddaughter or great-niece or whoever she was to betray a man like Ciano. To send a woman with those sympathies, those tastes, on such a mission – what idiots they were.'

'Good luck for us, sir, they got a lot of things wrong. But about the Duchess, sir? I was with her shortly after she heard of his execution. Couldn't we do something? She's had a pretty rum go.'

'It was a "low, dishonest decade" or hadn't you heard?'

'She did everything we asked of her, sir. She made an ass of Ribbentrop.'

'Not the world's toughest job.'

'You know what it cost her, and she never shed a tear. She was as cold as ice. She got thinner and paler and a lot older.' That was true. The mirror didn't lie. 'Please, sir, this would be a small thing. You should have seen her when we got the pictures from Milan.' Then Gordie began to talk about a woman I'd never heard of, Mary Postgate.[8] I thought she might have been an English girl assigned to keep watch on Gallo, to get the better of the German girl, possibly. I wondered who she was and how she'd wangled the job. I couldn't follow this part of the conversation at all.

At one point Willie said, 'Kipling knew a thing or two about women,' and Gordie replied, 'That's what Mary says, sir, despite all the rot that's talked about Lawrence.' Then they returned to the main topic, me, the Duchess of Windsor.

'Her Grace has suffered, sir. I think we owe her something.'

'Dulles would have a fit,' Willie said. 'He's gotten very solicitous of Edda.'

'I can understand that. It's good of him to protect a young widow who's been through all she's been through.'

'Not a bit of it, my boy. He's keeping her in reserve in case he needs to use her against the Communists. My enemy's enemy. You've no idea whom the Dulles brothers are thinking of bringing back from retirement. The Countess Ciano's Joan of Arc compared with some of them. More to the point, the diary's an historic document. We can't just insert something.'

'There were loose pages, sir, and I'm pretty good at handwriting.'

'I doubt she'd recognise his handwriting. He can't have been such a fool as to write to her.'

'Facsimiles might be published. She'd be sure to see those, but I'm pretty good, though I say it who shouldn't.' He certainly was good at handwriting. He'd written most of my husband's confidential correspondence for almost five years, and my most tiresome letters.

Maugham was silent for some time. I waited, standing very still, in the garden, trying not to make any crunching noises in the gravel path. 'There is something,' he said, 'that would mean nothing to anyone but her. If it came out, it could not possibly offend his widow. *Fortezza, Umilitade e Largo Core.* Try to find where it's from. It's Dante, not the *Commedia.* I've looked there myself. A few lines to go before and after should do the job.'

'Leave it to me, sir,' Gordie said. 'I'll do it up and I'll have some chaps I know make a photograph and I'll give it to her myself.'

We had a pleasant weekend with Maugham. It was becoming possible to get good food and wine again, and lunch on Sunday was almost what it might have been before the war. After Willie left, on Monday morning, I had a serious chat with Gordie. One of the things I liked so much about him was that he didn't look down on me when I asked him about something he must have known when he was nine. 'Who is Burckhardt?' was my first question.

'He was a great German Swiss scholar of the Italian Renaissance.'

'And who is Mary Postgate? And her father or grandfather, if he's important?'

This question troubled him. He'd mentioned the other name to me himself, but now he knew I'd overheard him with Willie.

' "Mary Postgate" is a short story, ma'am, by Rudyard Kipling, about the First World War. It's controversial. A lot of people disapprove of it. The title character loses someone dear to her, the only one she's ever loved, and when a German aviator crashes into her garden, she lets him bleed to death.'

'Really? Not very English, is it?' But very human, I thought.

'That's the point, and what people find really shocking is that she's a plain creature, a gentlewoman but a sort of servant, a paid companion, and afterwards, after the soldier dies, she looks radiant – "almost handsome" is the way another woman character, her employer, describes her.'

'Like she's had sex?'

'Possibly. I'm not sure Kipling meant to go as far as that.'

'Not quite the same, I'd say.' But good, I thought, damned good. And when Norman Birkett hanged Göring and Ribbentrop,[9] that would be good too.

A few weeks later, Gordie came to stay with us again. His fiancée was in Scotland with her parents for the last few weeks before their wedding. He took me out onto the terrace overlooking the sea. 'The sea's glorious today, isn't it? And the sky? The Bahamas are pleasant enough, but there's nothing like the Mediterranean.'

'Nothing,' I agreed with him. 'Nothing in the world.'

'I have something for you, Your Grace. It may be hard for you, but I thought about it and I felt it would be wrong, it would be more unkind, to keep it from you.' He was carrying a buff docket, the kind he had in Nassau, just like the one with the pictures of Mussolini's mutilated corpse. 'Along with Count Ciano's diaries, the Americans got some loose sheets, some torn from his date-books and some just jottings. This is a quatrain from a minor poem of Dante's. Mr Maugham recognised one of the lines as your school motto.'

'Please.' I held out my hand for it and my hand was shaking, although I knew it was a fraud.

There were four lines, and Willie was right, I had no idea what

Gallo's handwriting looked like. He didn't write me stupid drivelling letters, and besides, Gordie could fake my handwriting and the Duke's, so why not his?

I held it and looked at it and I knew I could never make any sense of it.

'Shall I read it to you?' Gordie asked, after waiting more than a decent interval. He was a very sweet boy.

'Yes, please.'

> '*Savere e cortesia, ingegno ed arte,*
> *nobilitate, bellezza e riccore,*
> *fortezza e umilitate e largo core,*
> *prodezza ed eccellenza, giunte e sparte.*' [10]

The third line was the Oldfields motto, the one I'd used to make an impression on Gallo that night in the palace in Rhodes. After I'd repeated those words, things began between us. I suppose the evening would have been much the same without it, but I felt it made a difference. He'd have taken me because he knew I wanted him, but he'd have taken me less seriously. 'What does it mean?'

'Well, very roughly, I'm a bit rusty: Learning and charm, wit and elegance, or possibly "glamour" might be better.'

' "Glamour"?' I had no idea there was a word for that so long ago.

'Yes, that's good, "glamour".

> . . . wit and glamour,
> nobility, beauty, and riches,
> fortitude, humility, and a generous heart,
> gallantry and glory, whether we are together or apart.

You see, the last bit, *giunte*, is like "joint", an old way of saying "together", and *sparte* is "separate" or "apart".' [11]

'Does it really mean that, "whether we are together or apart"?'

'Poetry can't be translated word for word. I'm giving the sense as best I can.'

'And what is "estate 1936"?'

'*Es-ta-te, millenovecentotrentasei*,' he said. 'Summer 1936.'

'Really? Are you sure?'

'Quite. I'm not so rusty that I don't know the names of the four seasons.'

He handed it back to me and I was happy to have it. I knew it was bogus, but a lot is in wartime.

Endnotes

CHAPTER ONE

1   Duchess of Windsor, *The Heart Has Its Reasons*, 40. This purports to be the Duchess's autobiography. She appears as a devoted daughter, popular debutante, eager bride, life of the party on several naval bases, abused wife, gallant divorcee, wife once more, determined-this-time-to-make-a-go-of-it. As the drama mounts, she is an Innocent Abroad swept off her feet by the Prince of Wales. In time, she becomes 'the woman I love,' imploring the King not to abandon his throne, his people, and his destiny, and so forth. It appears in subsequent citations as *Heart*.

2   Bloch, ed., *Wallis and Edward, Letters 1931–1936*. In these letters, one begins to get to know Wallis. She writes to Aunt Bessie Merryman, October 14, 1935: 'There is much war talk but I do hope this country won't be silly enough to become involved' (162–63). In an earlier letter, she confides her fears that the world is 'going to the bow-wows' (35). In subsequent citations, *Letters*.

CHAPTER TWO

1   *Letters*, 136. After the death of her mother, Aunt Bessie became her closest confidante. Despite the generation that separated them, and the decorum an older woman might have tried to encourage, they seem to be girls dishing the dirt with no secrets from each other. 'As bad taste as the clippings are do keep sending them.' Again, 'push the dirt along' (147).

2   Joseph P. Kennedy, *Hostage to Fortune: The Letters of Joseph P. Kennedy*, ed. by his granddaughter, Amanda Smith (New York: Viking, 2001), diary entry, April 14, 1939: 'I know of no job that I could occupy that might force my wife to dine with a tart' (326). This compunction, so insulting and so surprising in a man of Kennedy's ambition, is recalled as having been expressed to William Hillman,

chief foreign correspondent for the Hearst newspapers, 1934–39, and European manager of Hearst International News Service, 1936–39, so very likely Kennedy had announced it years earlier. Lord Halifax, no admirer of the Duchess, recalls, on July 19, 1940, having heard this 'coarse story.'

3 Culme and Rayner, *The Jewels of the Duchess of Windsor*, plates numbers 103 and 105. Her jewels and the furnishings of her house in Paris were auctioned by Sotheby's in 1987. Their sale raised $45 million for the Pasteur Institute for medical research, seven times the pre-sale estimate (7). The catalogue was subsequently published in book form.

4 Nicolson, *Diaries and Letters, 1930–1939*, 255, April 2, 1936. HN had observed a few months before, on January 13, 1936: 'I have an uneasy feeling that Mrs Simpson, in spite of her good intentions, is getting him out of touch with the type of person with whom he ought to associate . . . I think she is a nice woman who has flaunted suddenly into this absurd mess' (238). Diana Cooper, in *Light of Common Day*, expressed reservations about Mrs Simpson as hostess for the Prince: 'The food at dinner staggers and gluts . . . Social life . . . centres around the swimming pool . . . ' (161–62). I found Diana Cooper a joy, amusing, perceptive, sometimes acerbic, but never mean-spirited.

5 *Heart*, 8.

6 *Letters*, 90–91. Wallis toyed with the idea that her husband might have had Jewish ancestry, or indeed Jewish grandparents. Far more suggestive, she wrote, on March 16, 1936: 'Ernest went on to Germany [from Scandinavia where they had vacationed together] where I hope he won't be interned' (193).

7 Léon Blum, premier of France during the Popular Front, 1936–38. Arrested and tried by Vichy; held at Buchenwald, then at Dachau, and liberated in May 1945.

8 Speech to British Legion, summer 1935. Duke of Windsor, *A King's Story*, 253, recalls the acute displeasure of George V at his son's unsanctioned dabbling in foreign policy. The King reminded him of the important but severely limited role of the Royal Family in a constitutional monarchy.

9 Weitz, *Hitler's Diplomat*, 8.

10 Whalen, *Founding Father*, 179, suggests that US recognition of the Vatican may have formed part of these negotiations; also Maier, *The*

Kennedys, 123–28. Father Charles Coughlin's radio broadcasts reached an audience estimated at 40 million in the 1930s. He preached 'Social Justice' and, in Roosevelt's first term, 'The New Deal is Christ's deal.' Increasingly, however, his attacks on the rich, on bankers and capitalists, especially Jewish ones, eclipsed his concern for the poor, and he broke with the President, denouncing him simultaneously as a capitalist tool and a Bolshevik. Joseph P. Kennedy worked with Cardinal Spellman of New York and with Cardinal Pacelli, later Pope Pius XII, to silence him.

11 *Letters*, 26–32, tells of the documents provided to establish Mrs Simpson's innocence in the dissolution of her first marriage; 40–41, the dress borrowed from Thelma Furness and worn with faux aquamarine and crystal necklace and hair ornament; and 106, Lady Furness's involvement with Aly Khan.

CHAPTER THREE

1 Higham, *Duchess of Windsor*, 160–61. This book is not always reliable, but this seems a fair account of the events of July 16, 1936. A man, variously known as Jerome Bannigan and David Andrew Macmahon, an Irish resident of Glasgow, approached the King, who was mounted observing a military review. On that occasion Edward VIII had reprised his remarks to the British Legion: 'Humanity cries out for peace and for the assurance of peace.' A policeman attempted to wrest the gun from the assailant, who managed to hurl the gun under the King's horse.

2 In June, Eamon de Valera, President of Ireland, demanded a new constitution that would abolish the office of Governor General, who represented the King as head of state.

3 *Letters*, 199.

4 Bloch, *Secret File*, 259. The Duchess referred to the King's niece, later Elizabeth II, as 'Shirley Temple' and to her parents as 'Mr and Mrs Temple.' She also refers to the Duchess of York, later Queen Elizabeth, as 'Cookie.'

5 *Letters*, 76.

6 Nicholas Longworth, Speaker of the US House of Representatives (1925–31), married President Theodore Roosevelt's eldest daughter, Alice, then twenty-two, in 1906, when he was thirty-eight and already a Member of Congress. He died April 9, 1931. Neither was

monogamous.

7   It was rumoured that Wallis Spencer, married to a US naval officer posted to Hong Kong, conceived a child with Count Ciano in China and that her subsequent abortion left her infertile. She acknowledged an 'operation' in Seattle after leaving China (*Heart*, 120). However, the dates of their travels make it impossible for them to have met during those years. Wallis Warfield Spencer went to Hong Kong in 1924, left China in the summer of 1925 after some anti-British incidents in Peking, and never returned. Galeazzo Ciano did not enter the Italian diplomatic service until 1925, was sent first, for more than a year, to South America, and only then, in 1927, to China. He went back in 1930 after his marriage to Edda Mussolini. Moseley, *Mussolini's Shadow*, note, pp. 9–10, agrees that Ciano did not meet Wallis Spencer in China but confirms that they knew each other.

8   *Heart*, 96, Felipe Espil, an Argentine diplomat in Washington, who later became ambassador to the United States. She says they spoke of marriage, though it seems unlikely that an ambitious South American would have chosen a penniless Protestant divorcee. *Letters*, 45.

9   Duff Cooper, *Old Men Forget*, 189–94. The Coopers grew close, during this period, to Dino Grandi, the Italian ambassador. Diana Cooper, *Light of Common Day*, 167: 'Thanks to . . . wit and his true love for England, he weathered until the last day of peace the Abyssinian war . . . After all the alarms and tribulations Dino Grandi is still a treasured piece of what remains.' Dennis Mack Smith, with the advantage of hindsight and access to Italian archives, judged Grandi more harshly: 'Unfortunately, now as later, Grandi was chiefly concerned to flatter Mussolini into thinking that the British admired him excessively and were sufficiently hypocritical to support him in a war: if it came to the worst, they were a decadent race who could never stand up against the might of fascist Italy' (*Mussolini*, 192).

10 *Letters*, August 28, 1935, To Aunt Bessie: 'Your blue eyed charmer [the Prince of Wales] is the most disappointed small boy you can imagine. You would think Mussolini had planned this mess just to break up the yachting trip' (155).

11 *Letters*, 16: Syrie Maugham was associated with Elsie de Wolfe, Lady Mendl, whose book *The House in Good Taste* was influential in circles to which Mrs Simpson aspired.

12 Higham, *Duchess of Windsor*, 48–49.

13   *Heart*, 90–120. Wallis Spencer lived apart from her husband after the end of the First World War. He was sent to China in 1922 and they attempted a reconciliation, which was short-lived, in 1924. She lived with Herman and Katherine Rogers during most of the time she spent in China.

14   Edward, Prince of Wales, *Letters from a Prince*, March 23, 1920, To Freda Dudley Ward, his first acknowledged mistress: 'I hate to think of you travelling through France and Italy without me, beloved, for all those dirty little Frenchmen & unspeakable & revolting Dagoes to gaze & fall in love with . . . ' (301). The Prince was twenty-six years old when he wrote this letter, two years after the end of the Great War in which he served as an officer and in which France and Italy fought as Britain's allies.

15   Queen Elizabeth served as Colonel-in-Chief of the Black Watch for sixty-five years, from 1937 until her death in 2002.

16   *Duff Cooper Diaries*, 138–58. He was closely involved in negotiations that led to the end of the British Protectorate in 1922.

17   *Heart*, 111.

18   Unlike Duff and Diana Cooper, whose published memoirs give their impressions of the Duchess, the Whitmans never wrote about their acquaintance with her. I have changed their names to honour the reticence they maintained in their lifetime. Moreover, many of Mr Whitman's wartime exploits remain classified. Their daughter, who graciously agreed to speak with me, confided her mother's misgivings about 'renewing' a friendship that had never existed when she and Wallis Warfield were at school together. 'Mother's sense of duty as a citizen,' she recalled, 'overcame her scruples about social niceties.'

19   *Heart*, 66–67. Mary Kirk Raffray, who had been Wallis Warfield's bridesmaid when she married Lieutenant Win Spencer in 1916, caught the bouquet and married Captain Jacques Raffray, a French liaison officer, a year or so later. She married Ernest Simpson in 1937. 'Mary's clothes are rather naked for here' (*Letters*, 195).

20   *Letters*, 214. This may be a coincidence, but it strengthens my sense of the Duchess as a woman who never forgot or forgave.

CHAPTER FOUR

1   *Letters*, 121, Prince Paul of Yugoslavia: 'Mrs Simpson, there is no question about it – you are wearing the most striking dress in the

room.' The dress was designed by Eva Lutyens, the daughter of the prominent architect Sir Edwin Landseer Lutyens. Mrs Simpson meant to make an impression.

2 Lawrence Durrell, visiting in 1945, called it 'a design for a Neapolitan ice' and a 'thesis in totalitarian architecture' (*Prospero's Cell*, 28–29). I have been there too and seen the renovations.

3 Cooper, *Light of Common Day*, 178: 'The others never wear the same dress twice. I can't do that, of course, but mine are appropriate and sensible.'

4 Oldfields School was established in Glencoe, Maryland, in 1867 by Anna Austen McCulloch. 'Our motto – Fortezza, Umilitade, e Largo Core – Courage, Humility, and Largeness of Heart, are the core values and beliefs that define our school culture' (Oldfields school.org).

5 *Letters*, 217.

6 Higham, *Duchess of Windsor*, 163.

7 Edward, Duke of Windsor, *A King's Story*, 97.

8 Cooper, *Light of Common Day*, 182–83.

9 Ibid., 181. Diana Cooper said forty minutes and a glorious steep ascent, 'one endless flight of steps bordered by symmetrical cypresses . . .'

10 *Letters*, 65: 'The prince suggested those who preferred a more rigorous test of mental skill [more rigorous than cards] might try to put together an extremely complicated jig saw puzzle . . . ' A photograph of the King at work on such a puzzle during the *Nahlin* cruise can be found facing page 179 in *The Duff Cooper Diaries*.

11 Culme and Rayner, *Jewels*, no. 155.

12 Moseley, *Mussolini's Shadow*, 17–20. Ciano and two of Mussolini's sons flew in Abyssinia, an aerial campaign that included indiscriminate bombing of civilians and the use of poison gas. Il Duce attached enormous importance to aviation and had himself tried for a pilot's licence in the twenties, when an accident put an end to his flying lessons.

13 *Letters*, 118.

14 This line appears in a *tenzone*, a 'conversation' with another poet, Dante da Maiano, which dealt with Ovid's understanding of the relation between love and virtue, a question of perennial interest. I am grateful for the erudition of my friend Judith A. Kates, who found the poem. Ciano studied Latin and Greek in *liceo*. While a student at the

Sapienza University in Rome, he attempted journalism and, after graduating with a degree in law, published some short stories. Two of his plays, one a reworking of *Hamlet*, were produced with little success before his father urged or ordered him to try diplomacy. (Vergani, *Ciano*, 19–25; also Moseley, *Mussolini's Shadow*, 9–10.)

15 Galeazzo Ciano's feelings for Mussolini are described in a variety of ways. Renzo De Felice, who wrote the preface to the definitive Rizzoli edition of his *Diario*, believed that Ciano 'loved' him (xii). His friend and slightly older contemporary, the writer and photo-journalist Orio Vergani, in *Ciano: Una lunga confessione*, gave a somewhat more complicated sense of 'obedience' and admiration tempered by confidence in his own intelligence, 'a canniness that was Tuscan and particularly Livornese' (38: *Riconosceva a se stesso il solo privilegio di un'astuzia o, come lui stesso diceva, di una furbizia toscana e precisamente livornese*). Sumner Welles, in his introduction to the American edition of the diary, recalled that he had seen the Count, whom he described as a man who 'lacked neither personal dignity nor physical courage,' nonetheless 'quail' before Il Duce (xvii).

16 Ciano, *Diary*, February 25, 1938, wrote of von Hassel, German ambassador to Italy, 'I don't trust foreigners who know Dante. They want to screw us with poetry' (63).

17 *Jewels*, no. 104.

18 *Letters* confirms this usage, 213.

19 *Letters*, 92. *Heart*, 205, described King George V's official piper's praise for the prince's original composition.

20 *Heart*, 49.

21 The treaty was signed in London on August 27, 1936.

22 The piece does not appear in the Sotheby's catalogue, but many small items, including cufflinks belonging to the Duke, seem to have been lost.

CHAPTER FIVE

1 *Heart*, 80–81: 'I am naturally gay and flirtatious, and I was brought up to believe that one should be as entertaining as one can at a party.'

2 Culme and Rayner, *Jewels*, dust jacket, back cover, no number.

3 *Letters*, 57.

4 Daley, *Diana Mosley*. Jessica's elopement to Spain, 235–36; Diana's marriage to Mosley, 223–25.

Endnotes

5 Nicolson, *Diaries and Letters, 1930–1939*: biography of Dwight Morrow, 175–76; renting of Longbarn, 247.

6 *Letters*, 198.

7 Weitz, *Hitler's Diplomat*, 92. Weitz says Hitler himself asked Ribbentrop about it and, although it was dangerous to evade a direct question from the Führer, Ribbentrop declined to explain.

8 Graves and Hodges, *The Long Week-End*, 361. Graves, poet, novelist, and classicist, collaborated on this evocative contemporary history, first published in 1940.

9 *Letters*, 304: 'I don't know myself what is meant by a lobbyist.'

10 Cooper, *Light of Common Day*, 213.

11 Weitz, *Hitler's Diplomat*, 27–28.

12 Erwin Panofsky explored this question about Titian's *Bacchus and Ariadne* in *Problems in Titian, Mostly Iconographic*, 143–44.

13 Nicolson, *Diaries and Letters*: 'He looks young with a touch of arrested development' (132); 'an inspired mechanic' (180).

14 Scott Berg's *Lindbergh* provides an account of his father's congressional career (34–50) and of his own disrupted formal education, ending with his expulsion from the University of Wisconsin on academic grounds (60).

15 *Letters*, 210–11: 'I have been advised by Duff Cooper that a house is necessary.'

CHAPTER SIX

1 *Letters*, 232. William Norman Birkett, KC, Barrow-in-Furness Grammar School and Emmanuel College. He sat briefly, in the 1920s, as Liberal MP for Nottingham, and after a distinguished career in the law he was created first Baron Birkett in 1958.

2 October 27, 1936, the formal creation of the Rome-Berlin Axis.

3 *Letters*, 39: 'while I'm away the 4 servants eating their heads off.'

4 Maugham, *Ashenden*, 4.

5 *Duff Cooper Diaries*, January 20, 1936: 'I think she is a nice woman and a sensible woman – but she is as hard as nails and she does not love him' (228).

CHAPTER SEVEN

1 *Letters*, 242: 'His mother had finally completed her move into Marlborough House . . . and David, none too happily, was installed in Buckingham Palace.'

2 Lindbergh, *Flower and Nettle*. 'Ah yes – the subservience of women in Germany!' (83); Rilke problem (185).

3 Ibid., 82.

4 Ibid., AML's recollections of both, 97–98.

5 *Letters*, 239–45.

6 *Heart*, 251–52.

7 Duff Cooper gave a chivalrous account of this conversation in his memoir, *Old Men Forget*, 201–2: 'I then suggested a postponement . . . I also secretly thought that he might in the interval meet somebody whom he would love more. He never has.'

8 John Buchan, created Lord Tweedsmuir in 1935, was the son of a minister in the Free Church of Scotland. Legend has it that he walked six miles a day to his first school. Subsequently he attended grammar school in Glasgow, Glasgow University, and Brasenose College, Oxford. Barrister, soldier, writer and publisher, MP for the Scottish Universities, he wrote more than a hundred works of fiction, history, and biography.

9 Graves and Hodges, *The Long Week-End*, 364–65.

10 Smith, *Mussolini*, 217, notes strong ties between Fascist Italy and Chiang prior to 1937.

11 *Heart*, 45: 'The thought of going to college never occurred to me – it just didn't exist for girls of my upbringing. In fact, not a single girl from my class at Oldfields went to college.' This was not so. Polly Parsons Whitman went to a women's college in New England and graduated with High Honours in History and Classics.

12 Maier, *The Kennedys*, 116.

CHAPTER EIGHT

1 Graves and Hodges, *The Long Week-End*, 361–62.

2 *Letters*, 244–45.

3 *Heart*, 267.

4 Ibid., 266–68.

5 Nicolson, *Diaries and Letters*, 304–7. Nicolson retrieved these papers in the fall of 1937 and arranged for them to be sent to the Duchess,

then honeymooning in Austria. *Heart,* 268: the Duchess thanks him for it.

6   *Heart,* 280; *Letters,* 308.

7   *Letters,* 261, December 12, 1936.

8   Graves and Hodges, *The Long Week-End,* 365.

9   *Letters,* 116.

10 Morton, *Rothschilds,* 253–55.

CHAPTER NINE

1   Higham, *Duchess of Windsor,* 208; *Heart,* 291.

2   Culme and Rayner, *Jewels,* no. 110.

3   Ibid., no. 98.

4   *Letters,* 270.

5   *Letters,* 14 December 1936, 264.

6   *Time,* January 1937; *Time,* January 1928; *Time,* January 1936; *Time,* January 1938.

7   *Letters:* first mention of WE, 'WE must hold each other so tight. It will all work out for us. God bless WE' (171); design for writing paper, January 1, 1937 (274).

8   *Letters,* 290–91, February 6, 1937.

9   Morton, *Rothschilds,* family tree. Kitty Wolf, b. 1885; divorced Graf Schönborn-Bucheim, and married Baron Eugène de Rothschild in 1925.

10 *Letters,* 321–22.

11 Ibid., 222–24.

12 Weitz, *Hitler's Diplomat,* 128–29.

13 *Letters,* 328–29.

14 Daley, *Diana Mosley,* 144–45.

15 Higham, *Duchess of Windsor,* 231.

16 Ibid., 237.

CHAPTER TEN

1   *Heart,* 308–9.

2   Ibid., 310.

3   Culme and Rayner, *Jewels,* documents the Duchess's remarkable collection of rubies, nos. 131–39.

4   Edward, Prince of Wales, *Letters from a Prince:* July 10, 1920, 'the most revolting form of living creatures I've ever seen!! . . . & the

nearest things to monkeys I've ever seen' (348); and Samoa, August 25, 'very trying day ashore . . . anyway trying to me, sweetie, who just loathes natives & native stunts' (374).

5 Smith, *Mussolini*, 20. Margherita Sarfatti herself published a less critical biography, *Dux*, in 1925, which was eventually translated into eighteen languages. She compared Mussolini to Julian the Apostate, Cromwell, Washington, Dick Whittington, and Tom Sawyer. More pointedly, she contrasted him with Lenin: two leaders had arisen in the early years of the new century, one representing 'the desolation of the steppes,' the other 'the beneficence of the Italian sun: . . . one had come to demolish, the other to reconstruct' (19). Though obviously besotted with him, she presented their relationship as formal and collegial. They worked together, first on the Socialist paper *Avanti* and then, after the Fascists burned its offices, on Mussolini's own *Il Popolo d'Italia*. She addressed him as *Direttore*; he called her *Signora*. She took pains to assure her readers that the fire injured no one, but sufficed to destroy the building and the presses (128). She wanted them to know, too, that she befriended Mussolini at the urging of her husband, Cesare Sarfatti, a prominent lawyer and civil libertarian, who first saw him at a Socialist Party conference in 1912: 'a wonderful young man . . . most original . . . a great future before him' (176).

6 Edda Ciano, *My Truth*, 70. The Countess herself later wrote that her husband intervened to free her 'boyfriend' and his father from internment. 'He did so immediately, not only to please me but also because he felt they had done nothing against Italy and should be freed.'

7 This man, I assume, is most likely Albert Kesselring, then chief of the Luftwaffe General Staff. He was made commander of German forces in Italy in 1943, where he was responsible for many civilian deaths in reprisal for partisan attacks. His reputation for pro-Italian sympathies rests, presumably, upon his efforts to spare the artistic treasures of Florence, Siena, and Orvieto.

8 Welles, *Time for Decision*, 113: 'His hands were shaped like the digging claws of a badger.'

9 Weitz, *Hitler's Diplomat*, 118.

10 Ibid., 143–44 (Ambassador's Report A5522).

11 Lindbergh, *Flower and Nettle*, 84ff.

12 *Letters*, 203.

1 Letter of December 22, 1937, written from Lou Viei, *Guardian* on-line archive.

2 Culme and Rayner, *Jewels*, no. 182.

3 *Heart*, 313.

4 *Blithe Spirit: The Windsor Set*, Metropolitan Museum of Art, November 1, 2002–February 9, 2003, displayed many of these dresses, as well as the Duchess's Mainbocher wedding dress.

5 Weitz, *Hitler's Diplomat*, 158.

6 *Los Angeles Times*, March 10, 2001. Maria Altman, then eighty-five, niece of Adele Bloch-Bauer, told Anne-Marie O'Connor, a staff writer, about the violin, the painting, and the necklace. The portrait is now in New York at the Neue Gallerie. The necklace has never been recovered and perhaps, as the Duchess came to suspect, the stones have been reset.

7 Ciano, *Diary*, February 13, 1938: 'I believe she is one of the very few women capable of making a good impression for us abroad' (57).

8 Queen Elizabeth's White Wardrobe went on exhibit at Buckingham Palace in July 2005. See also Lacey, *Queen Mother's Century*, 70–71.

9 *Blithe Spirit* included this dress.

10 In Livorno.

11 *Guides Bleus, Des Alpes à Rome*, 102.

12 Moseley, *Mussolini's Shadow*, 58–59. Mussolini, returning Duff Cooper's *Talleyrand*, borrowed from his son-in-law, is said to have told him, 'I must conclude that when he seeks only beautiful women and terrible books, decadence for a man is certain.'

13 Winston Churchill did not reach precisely this conclusion, but he wrote: 'The association is psychical rather than sexual, and certainly not sensual except incidentally.' Martin Gilbert, *Winston Churchill*, vol. V (London: Heinemann, 1976), 810; quoted by Michael Bloch in *Letters*, 127.

14 Ciano, *Diary*, 151. Sumner Welles had the same impression, 'a white tunic on which were plastered various emblems and insignia in brilliants . . . On his right hand he wore an enormous ring set with six huge diamonds. On his left he wore an emerald at least an inch square' (*Time for Decision*, 113). William Shirer noted in *Berlin Diary* that at the mass meeting during which Göring, seated on the stage,

was made a Field Marshal, he kept opening the box that held his new insignia and gloating over it (456).

CHAPTER TWELVE

1 Lindbergh, *Flower and Nettle*, gives a lengthy description of this dinner party and provides a guest list (501–11).

2 Culme and Rayner, *Jewels*, no. 189.

3 Ibid., no. 179.

4 Berg, *Lindbergh*, 370–74.

5 Lindbergh, *Flower and Nettle*, 504.

6 Paul Reynaud (1878–1956) became foreign minister in 1938 and the last premier of the Third Republic in March 1940. He served until the surrender on June 16, 1940. He was arrested shortly thereafter by Vichy authorities and sent to Germany, where he was imprisoned for the duration of the war. He was liberated by Allied forces in May 1945.

7 Lindbergh, *Flower and Nettle*, 505–6.

8 Ibid., 510.

9 Whalen, *Founding Father*. Harvard-Yale game, 1937 (228), Harvard commencement, 1938 (228–29).

10 David McCord, *In Sight of Sever*, 17–19, wrote of Lord Tweedsmuir's honorary degree and recalled an earlier visit to New England when he spoke of 'The Two Ordeals of Democracy,' the US Civil War and the Great War, at Milton Academy. John Buchan's World War I novels are *The Thirty-Nine Steps, Greenmantle*, and *Mr Standfast*. He also wrote a 24-volume history of the war.

11 Pearl Buck, *Other Gods*, went through three printings in 1938, 1939, and 1940. A shortened version appeared in *Good Housekeeping* as 'An American Legend.'

12 Lindbergh, *Flower and Nettle*, 507–10.

13 Berg, *Lindbergh*, 377–80; and Lindbergh, *Flower and Nettle*, 437.

14 Buck, *Other Gods*, 4.

15 Ibid., 5.

16 Ibid., 142.

17 Ibid., 328.

18 Berg, *Lindbergh*, 192–93. He met Anne Morrow in 1928, when he was twenty-six years old. Prior to that, 'by his own admission, America's most eligible bachelor "had never been enough interested in any girl to ask her to go on a date".'

19 Bloch, *Duke of Windsor's War*, 10.

20 Cooper, *Old Men Forget*, 251.

21 Cooper, *Talleyrand*, 162.

22 Lindbergh, *Flower and Nettle*, 564–65. Anne Lindbergh wrote of the Baroness: 'She is bitter, tired, and disillusioned, but with real force and a great deal of intelligence. "I no longer love – or hate".'

CHAPTER THIRTEEN

1 Count Alexandre Walewski, 1810–1868, served as ambassador to London and as foreign minister of France during the Second Empire.

2 Friedel, *Franklin D. Roosevelt*, 317.

3 *Time*, July 24, 1939.

4 Ciano, *Diary*, 257–58, August 11–13, 1939. He spoke of Mussolini 'letting me go,' but believed that Il Duce, at that time, also wished to avoid war. He found Ribbentrop 'evasive, he has lied to me too many times,' and concluded that, with Hitler, 'the decision to fight is implacable . . . I am certain that even if the Germans were given more than they ask for they would attack just the same, because they are possessed by the demon of destruction.'

5 Bloch, *Duke of Windsor's War*, 11–12, describes this episode: the telegrams, the leak, and the replies, and the Duke's satisfaction that he had helped preserve Italian neutrality.

6 *Heart*, 326–29.

7 Ibid., 208–9.

8 Minney, *Private Papers of Hore-Belisha*, 236–39. Hore-Belisha recalled the King's distress at the prospect of the Duke's visiting troops with the Duchess. 'He seemed very disturbed and walked up and down the room. He said the Duke never had any discipline in his life.' H.-B. promised the King that he would see the Duke himself and 'arrange matters so that he need not come into it at all.'

9 Lacey, *Queen Mother's Century*, 75.

10 Culme and Rayner, *Jewels*, no. 115.

11 *Heart*, 342.

12 Cooper, *Old Men Forget*, 275; Bloch, *Duke of Windsor's War*, 61.

13 Published as *Sick Heart River* in Britain and as *Mountain Meadow* in the United States, the book told of the death in Canada of Buchan's fictional alter ego, Sir Edward Leithen. He dies confident that the 'free peoples' will, once more, defeat the 'slave peoples,' but with

great sacrifice (250). The book begins with a couplet from the *Proverbs of Alfred*: 'If thou hast a woe tell it not to the weakling / Tell it to thy saddle-bow, and ride forth singing' (1).

14 Berg, *Lindbergh*, Chapter 14, 'The Great Debate,' 384–432.

15 Wheeler, *Yankee from the West*, 353–67, deals largely with the domestic politics of the 1940 convention. He claims to have refused the vice-presidential nomination.

16 Berg, *Lindbergh*, 390–93.

17 Saint-Exupéry, *Terre*, 61: '*Sa grandeur, c'est de se sentir responsable.*' Anne Lindbergh greatly admired the English version, *Wind, Sand, and Stars*.

18 Hilaire Belloc, *Ladies and Gentlemen* (London: Duckworth, 1932), 15–17. First appeared in *The New Statesman*.

19 Bloch, *Duke of Windsor's War*, 62.

20 Ibid., 66–68.

21 Panter-Downes, *London War Notes*, 64, June 2, 1940.

CHAPTER FOURTEEN

1 Richard Cobb, Balliol's great historian of the French Revolution, a passionate francophile who studied in Paris in the 1930s, described the 'fantastic, limpid, derisively beautiful summer of 1940' as refugees fled the Germans, seeking safety in unoccupied France and beyond ('L'Exode and After' in *Promenades*, 54).

2 Panter-Downes, *London War Notes*, 67–68.

3 Bloch, *Duke of Windsor's War*, 71.

4 Ibid., 72–75.

5 Ibid., 88, the Caliph's Palace in Ronda.

6 Ibid., 83.

7 'The children won't go without me. I won't leave the King. And the King will never leave.'

8 Lacey, *Queen Mother's Century*, 72.

9 Nicolson, *Letters and Diaries, 1939–1945*, 100: 'She is being instructed every morning how to fire a revolver.' *Letters, 1930–1939*, 405: 'one of the most amazing queens since Cleopatra.'

10 Edward, Duke of Windsor, *A King's Story*, 260: 'my intended wife was beyond reproach under the law . . . '

11 Bloch, *Duke of Windsor's War*, 93.

12 Ibid., 91–94.

13 In 1937, Pope Pius XI issued an encyclical. *Mit Brennender Sorge, With Burning Sorrow*, attacking Nazi racism as a form of idolatry and explicitly grounding Christian doctrine in the 'sacred books of the Old Testament [which] are exclusively the word of God and constitute a substantial part of his revelation.' Pius XII took a considerably less confrontational position with regard to the Third Reich.

14 Whalen, *Founding Father*, 261–62; Maier, *The Kennedys*, 123–28.

15 Ciano, *Diary*, 233.

16 Whalen, *Founding Father*, 263.

17 Ibid., 303–5. See also Beschloss, *Kennedy and Roosevelt*, 193–222.

18 Sumner Welles was punctilious in thanking Kennedy for this (*Time for Decision*, 129–30).

19 It was mutual: Welles said of Ribbentrop, 'The pomposity and absurdity of his manner could not be exaggerated' (*Time for Decision*, 92).

20 Benjamin Sumner Welles chose to be called Sumner to emphasise his kinship with Charles Sumner, an abolitionist beaten almost to death on the floor of the Senate by a Southern congressman in 1856 during the crisis over 'Bloody Kansas.' Massachusetts re-elected him the same year, when his survival remained in doubt, so that his empty chair might remain as a reproach to the slave-holders. He was able to return to the Senate in 1859 and served throughout the Civil War and Reconstruction. Welles was related also to Edith Wharton.

21 In *The Time for Decision*, 78–83, Sumner Welles recalled Ciano as 'cordial and entirely unaffected. He could not have been simpler or more outspoken in the expression of his views.' Welles told Ciano that Washington had closely followed his efforts the previous August to prevent war. Ciano 'made no effort to conceal his hearty detestation of Ribbentrop.' Further, he said, 'No country would wish to have Germany for a neighbour.' And again, Ciano expressed 'his hatred and contempt for Ribbentrop but also an underlying antagonism for Hitler.' Welles recalled, however, his own conviction early in 1940 that although 'the vast majority of the Italian people – also key figures within the Italian government itself – totally and even violently opposed the entry of Italy into the war,' Mussolini alone would determine Italy's action. On December 31, 1939, Ciano had concluded that Mussolini would almost certainly choose to fight with Germany, 'against the democracies . . . the only countries with which one can deal honestly and seriously' (*Diary*, 307).

22 Ciano, *Diary*, 314, January 21, 1940: 'Countess Potocka, with whom I went hunting wild boar last year in Bialowieza and whom I was instrumental in freeing from a Russian prison some weeks ago, came to see me. She described with dignity her life in Russia during her imprisonment, her return trip, and her encounter with the Germans of the Gestapo. She wishes neither to alarm me nor to seek my pity. She is too aristocratic (*molta razza*) for that. She despises the Russians. She hates the Germans.' As to relations with the Russians, Ciano got on well with Lev Helfand, the Soviet *chargé*, whom he describes as 'refined and intelligent' (7). Of Jewish origin, he was recalled to Moscow, July 14, 1940, where Ciano sensed 'he can smell the whiff of the firing squad.' He asked Ciano to help his family escape to the United States. Ciano said Helfand feared their deportation more than his own death, and found Helfand's love for his family 'very human and very beautiful' (370–71). With the help of the American ambassador also, the family made its way to New York, where they took the surname Moore. Helfand's wife, Sonia Moore (1902–1995), was an actress who helped to introduce the Stanislavski method in the United States. See Sonia Moore, *Training an Actor: The Stanislavski System in Class* (New York: Viking Press, 1979).

23 Bloch, *Duke of Windsor's War*, 86–87, correspondence between German ambassador and Ribbentrop. At the same time, the Spanish press published rumours that the Duke had broken with Churchill and his government and hoped to make peace with Germany.

24 Cooper, *Talleyrand*, 198–202.

CHAPTER FIFTEEN

1 *Heart*, 355.

2 Bloch, *Duke of Windsor's War*, 107–21.

3 See *Beyond the Chindwin* by Bernard Fergusson, an officer in the Black Watch and later Lord Ballantrae, Governor General of New Zealand. He mastered the Maori language, as he had previously learned Burmese tribal languages, and one of the two lessons read at his memorial service in London was in Maori.

4 This is, of course, Madeleine Bassett, who, curiously enough, was loved by Sir Roderick Spode, the 'black-shorted' (*sic*) leader of the BUF-like Saviours of Britain. See *The Code of the Woosters*.

5   Bloch, *Duke of Windsor's War*, 125: 'the most thoroughly hideous house I have ever seen.'

6   Berg, *Lindbergh*, 405–6.

7   Ibid., 407.

8   Whalen, *Founding Father*, 311–20.

9   Ibid., 330–36.

10   Nicolson, *Diaries and Letters, 1939–1945*, 125, November 6, 1940: 'My heart leapt like a young salmon when I heard that Roosevelt had won so triumphantly.'

11   *Heart.* The Duchess described her charitable efforts (354, 361–62).

12   Bloch, *Duke of Windsor's War*, 183–84.

13   Genesis 20: 1–16.

14   Bloch, *Duke of Windsor's War*, 217.

15   Ibid., 207–20.

16   *Heart*, 356–57.

17   Bloch, *Duke of Windsor's War*, 196–97, 230–33.

CHAPTER SIXTEEN

1   Moseley, *Mussolini's Shadow*, 155–67. In late January 1943, Allen W. Dulles, 'special assistant' to the US ambassador in Bern, in fact head of the OSS, the Office of Strategic Services, in Switzerland, began to hear of an anti-German group forming in Italy: Marshal Pietro Badoglio, Dino Grandi, former ambassador to Britain, and Ciano himself. Mussolini, doubtless, was aware of this also. Ciano's *Diary*, January and early February 1943, expressed the conviction that Germany had lost the war (580–88). The Nazis could not recover from Stalingrad and other reverses, but the Duce continued to be 'optimistic' about his allies. On February 5, 1943, Ciano wrote that the Duce, 'very embarrassed,' told him he was 'changing his entire cabinet' and that he could not continue as foreign minister. He offered Albania, which Ciano declined, and the post of ambassador to the Holy See, which he accepted. Ciano admitted feeling the 'anguish of his removal,' but resolved to 'look to tomorrow, *which may require even greater freedom of action*' (italics added). The penultimate entry in Count Ciano's *Diary*, February 8, 1943, recorded his attempts, again, to convince Mussolini of German treachery. It concludes: 'Our leave-taking was cordial, for which I am very glad, because I like Mussolini, like him very much ['*a Mussolini voglio bene,*

molto bene,' Diario, 697], and what I shall miss the most will be my contact with him.'

2   Cooper, *Operation Heartbreak.*

3   Smith, *Mussolini,* 294. The Fascist Grand Council, meeting July 24–25, 1943, voted 18–7 to restore to the King and Parliament the powers vested in them by 'the law and the constitution.' Moseley, *Mussolini's Shadow,* 168–73, gives a melodramatic account of the meeting: Many of the councillors were armed, Grandi himself possibly with hand grenades. Mussolini presided and spoke for two hours. Then, after other speeches, including Ciano's insisting that Italy must free itself from Germany, Mussolini himself demanded a vote, taken individually, by voice. Ciano voted with seventeen others to end his rule.

4   Moseley, *Mussolini's Shadow,* 178.

5   Ibid., 234–36, January 11, 1944. Dennis Mack Smith (*Mussolini,* 303–5) writes that the Nazis wanted to 'punish' Ciano but that the demand for his execution came from Fascist militants, *gerachi,* ashamed, he suggests, of having fled after the vote of July 25. They warned Mussolini against clemency and threatened to kill Ciano themselves if he would not. Mussolini ordered the trial and the verdict, and both the trial and the executions were filmed by the propaganda services. Mussolini subsequently drew up a list of two hundred other traitors to be arrested. Duff Cooper (*Old Men Forget,* 319) recalled that the news reached the British the next day. 'Winston was in a bad mood when de Gaulle arrived and was not very welcoming. He had just heard of the shooting of Ciano, Bono etc. which had rather shocked him.' Gaston Palewski accompanied de Gaulle, and Diana Cooper and Mrs Churchill joined them for lunch.

6   Psalm 57 is associated with David's flight from his father-in-law, King Saul, who sought to kill him.

CHAPTER SEVENTEEN

1   Higham, *Duchess of Windsor,* 381–82. Charles Glass, *Americans in Paris: Life and Death Under Nazi Occupation 1940–44,* has much to say about Bedaux's dealings with the Nazis and with Vichy.

2   See Raleigh Trevelyan, *The Fortress,* for a young man's story of the Anzio landing and its aftermath.

3   See Roger Heskith, *Fortitude: The D-Day Deception Campaign.*

4   Moseley, *Mussolini's Shadow,* 236.

CHAPTER EIGHTEEN

1 William Norman Birkett did indeed serve as one of three British judges at the Nuremberg trials.

2 Heskith, *Fortitude*. epigraph, from Francis Bacon, 'Essay on Vainglory': 'It was prettily devised of Æsop, The fly sat upon the axle-tree of the chariot wheel, and said, What a dust do I raise! So are there some vain persons, that whatsoever goeth alone or moveth upon greater means, if they have never so little hand in it, they think it is they that carry it.'

3 Welles wrote in his introduction to Ciano's *Diary*, xvii: 'Of all the men possessing high authority within the Axis governments, he was the only one who made it clear to me, without subterfuge and without hesitation, that he had opposed the war, that he continued to oppose the war, that he foresaw nothing but utter devastation for the whole of Europe through the extension of the war, and that every effort which he personally could undertake would be exerted to prevent the entrance of Italy into the conflict.'

4 Dino Grandi went to Portugal; Marshal Badoglio's prestige was such that he was able to replace Mussolini as prime minister and remain in Rome. Duff Cooper speculated, in July 1944, that the King and Badoglio plotted with Ciano and Grandi to remove Mussolini and, that accomplished, double-crossed them (*Duff Cooper Diaries*, 315).

5 Welles saw the diary in 1940 and heard passages read aloud by Ciano. He ridiculed Ribbentrop's notion that the Count kept two different versions: 'There is no question of its authenticity, nor have I any reason to believe that in the last tragic days . . . he had the opportunity or the desire to make any changes in what he had previously written' (Introduction to *Diary*, xviii). The CIA, successor to the wartime OSS, declassified the papers connected with the race, led by Allen Dulles, to secure the notebooks and keep them from the Germans (CIA Historical Review Program, 'Release in full, 22 September 93'). Available on-line at www.cia.gov/library/center-for-the-study-of-intelligence/kent-csi/docs/v.1312. The CIA history refers to Diulio Susmel's report (*La Via sbagliata di Galeazzo Ciano*, 333) that some Germans, Himmler among them, thought these records sufficiently important to consider making such a deal, but that Ribbentrop informed Hitler, who forbade it.

6 Ciano knew of his wife's efforts and acknowledged her 'in my hours of sorrow . . . a strong, reliable, and faithful companion' (*Diary*, 591). Edda Ciano (*My Truth*, 212–33) described her efforts, with the help of Marchese Emilio Pucci, to smuggle the papers to Switzerland. She used the threat of delivering them to the Allies in a futile attempt to bargain with her father for her husband's life. She noted the German woman as a 'shining example of loyalty' (225). 'People have claimed that she acted as she did because she was in love with Galeazzo. Certainly, but of what importance were feelings – or my reactions to this – when the life of my husband was at stake?' Countess Carolina Ciano recalled that Hildegarde Burckhardt Beetz brought her some of her son's belongings and confided to her that he had been 'the great love of her life' (Moseley, *Mussolini's Shadow*, 238). Frau Beetz, whose husband died on the eastern front, denied ever having met the elder countess. I have been unable to confirm Somerset Maugham's surmise that she was related to the historian.

7 The last entry in his *Diary*, written in Verona on December 23, 1943, revealed that at the Berchtesgaden meeting in August 1939, 'Hitler went so far as to tell me that I, a man of the South, could not comprehend how much he, as a Germanic man, needed to grab the timber in the Polish forests . . . ' (590).

8 Rudyard Kipling, 'Mary Postgate' (1915) in *The Works of Rudyard Kipling*, vol. 26, *A Diversity of Creatures* (New York: Charles Scribner's Sons, 1925), 489–513.

9 Göring committed suicide on October 15, 1946; Ribbentrop was hanged the next day.

10 Dante, 'Poems of Correspondence,' Dante da Maiano to Dante Alighieri: 'Love causes me to love so faithfully' (*Amor mi fa sí fedelmente amare*). Dante Alighieri's Reply: 'Knowledge and kindness, intellect and art' (*Savere e cortesia, ingegno ed arte*).

11 Lieutenant Wallingford-Just is translating the last line very freely.

Bibliography

Berg, A. Scott. *Lindbergh.* New York: G. P. Putnam's Sons, 1998.

Beschloss, Michael. *Kennedy and Roosevelt: The Uneasy Alliance.* New York: W. W. Norton, 1980.

Bloch, Michael. *The Duke of Windsor's War.* London: Weidenfeld and Nicolson, 1982.

—, ed. *The Intimate Correspondence of the Duke and Duchess of Windsor: Wallis and Edward, Letters 1931–1937.* New York: Avon, 1986.

—. *The Secret File of the Duke of Windsor.* New York: Bantam Press, 1988.

Buchan, John. *Mountain Meadow.* New York: The Literary Guild of America, 1940 and 1941.

Buck, Pearl. *Other Gods.* New York: The John Day Company, 1938. The third edition notes that a shorter version of this book was serialised in *Good Housekeeping* as 'An American Legend.'

Central Intelligence Agency. *The Ciano Papers: Rose Garden.* CIA Historical Review Program, Release in full: 22 September 1993.

Ciano, Edda. *My Truth.* New York: William Morrow, 1977.

Ciano, Galeazzo. *Diario, 1937–1943.* Milan: Rizzoli Editore, 1980.

—. *Diary 1937–1943.* New York: Doubleday, 1946, with introduction by Sumner Welles. New US edition: New York: Enigma Books, 2002. British edition: *Ciano's Diary, 1937–1943.* Introduction by Malcolm Muggeridge. London: Heinemann, 1947. London: Phoenix Press, 2002. The text of both of the newer English editions is based on the definitive 1980 Rizzoli volume, edited by Renzo De Felice, and both include his Preface.

Cobb, Richard. *Promenades.* Oxford: Oxford University Press, 1980.

Cooper, Diana. *The Light of Common Day.* London: Century Publishing, 1984. First published 1959 by Rupert Hart-Davis.

Cooper, Duff [Lord Norwich]. *The Duff Cooper Diaries, 1915–1951.* Edited and introduced by John Julius Norwich. London: Weidenfeld & Nicolson, 2005.

—. *Old Men Forget: The Autobiography of Duff Cooper.* London: Rupert Hart-Davis, 1953.

—. *Operation Heartbreak.* London: Rupert Hart-Davis, 1950.

—. *Talleyrand.* Bedford Historical Series. London: Jonathan Cape, 1938. First published 1932.

Culme, John, and Nicholas Rayner. *The Jewels of the Duchess of Windsor.* New York: The Vendome Press in association with Sotheby's, 1987.

Daley, Jan. *Diana Mosley.* New York: Alfred A. Knopf, 2000.

Durrell, Lawrence. *Prospero's Cell and Reflections on a Marine Venus.* New York: E. P. Dutton, 1962.

Edward, Prince of Wales [Duke of Windsor]. *Letters from a Prince, March 1919–January 1921.* Edited by Rupert Godfrey. London: Little, Brown, 1998.

Fergusson, Bernard. *Beyond the Chitwind.* London: Collins, 1945.

Freidel, Frank, *Franklin D. Roosevelt: A Rendezvous with Destiny.* Boston: Little, Brown, 1990.

Glass, Charles. *Americans in Paris: Life and Death under Nazi Occupation 1940–44.* London: Harper Press, 2009.

Graves, Robert, and Alan Hodge. *The Long Week-End: A Social History of Great Britain, 1918–1939.* New York: W. W. Norton, 1963. First published 1940.

Guides Bleus. Italie. Vol. 1, *Des Alpes à Rome.* Paris: Hachette, 1926.

Heskith, Roger. *Fortitude: The D-Day Deception Campaign.* New York: Overlook Press, 2000.

Higham, Charles. *The Duchess of Windsor: The Secret Life.* New York: Charter Books, 1988.

Lacey, Robert. *The Queen Mother's Century.* London: Little, Brown, 1999.

Lindbergh, Anne Morrow. *The Flower and the Nettle: Letters and Diaries, 1938–1939.* New York: Harcourt Brace Javonovitch, 1976.

Maier, Thomas, *The Kennedys: America's Emerald Kings.* New York: Basic Books, 2003

Maugham, Somerset. *Ashenden, or The British Agent.* Reprinted in series Best Mysteries of All Time. Pleasantville, NY: ImPress, 2006. First published 1927.

Bibliography

McCord, David. *In Sight of Sever*. Cambridge, MA: Harvard University Press, 1963.

Minney, R. J. *The Private Papers of Hore-Belisha*. London: Collins, 1960.

Morton, Frederick. *The Rothschilds: A Family Portrait*. New York: Atheneum, 1962.

Moseley, Ray. *Mussolini's Shadow: The Double Life of Count Galeazzo Ciano*. New Haven and New York: Yale University Press, 1999.

Nicolson, Harold. *Diaries and Letters*. Edited by Nigel Nicolson. Volume I, *1930–1939*. New York: Atheneum, 1966. Volume II, *The War Years, 1939–1945*. New York: Atheneum, 1967.

Panter-Downes, Mollie. *London War Notes, 1939–1945*. New York: Farrar, Straus and Giroux, 1971.

Saint-Exupéry, Antoine de. *Terre des Hommes*. Paris: Gallimard, 1939.

Sarfatti, Margherita G. *The Life of Benito Mussolini*. Translated by Frederic Whyte. London: Thornton Butterworth, 1925.

Smith, Dennis Mack. *Mussolini*. New York: Alfred A. Knopf, 1982.

Trevelyan, Raleigh. *The Fortress: A Diary of Anzio and After*. London: Buchan & Enright, 1956.

Vergani, Orio. *Ciano: Una lunga confessione*. Milan: Longanesi, 1974.

Weitz, John. *Hitler's Diplomat: The Life and Times of Joachim von Ribbentrop*. New York: Ticknor & Fields, 1992.

Welles, Sumner. *The Time for Decision*. New York: Harper & Brothers, 1944.

Whalen, Richard. *The Founding Father: The Story of Joseph P. Kennedy*. New York: New American Library, 1964.

Wheeler, Burton K. *Yankee from the West*. Garden City, NY: Doubleday, 1962.

Windsor, Edward, Duke of. *A King's Story: The Memoirs of the Duke of Windsor*. New York: G. P. Putnam's Sons, 1947.

Windsor, Wallis, Duchess of. *The Heart Has Its Reasons*. New York: Award Books, 1956.

Photo Credits

Mrs Ernest Simpson, presented at Court, June 10, 1931 (Popperfoto, Getty Images)

H.R.H. Edward, Prince of Wales, Colonel in the Welsh Guards (Hugh Cecil, Hulton Archive, Getty Images)

Sir Harold Nicolson (Wolfgang Suschitzky, National Portrait Gallery, London)

Duff Cooper, 1st Viscount Norwich (Bassano, National Portrait Gallery, London)

William Somerset Maugham (Bassano, National Portrait Gallery, London)

Andrew McMahon (Jerome Bannigan) apprehended July 16, 1936, in alleged attempt to assassinate Edward VIII (Ernest Brooks, Hulton Archive, Getty Images)

The King, Wallis Simpson, and Katherine Rogers ashore during cruise of the Nahlin (Hulton Archive, Getty Images)

Count Galeazzo Ciano, Shanghai, 1932 (The author believes this picture to be in the public domain. If rights are claimed, she asks that the holder(s) make themselves known so they may be acknowledged in future editions of this book)

Col. and Mrs Lindbergh with Herman Göring, Karinhall, July 28, 1936 (*Bildarchiv, Fotoarchiv Hoffmann, Bayerische Staatsbibliothek*, Munich)

The Duke of Windsor, Schloss Enzesfeld, December 1936 (Popperfoto, Getty Images)

Woman of the Year (*Time* magazine, January 4, Time Inc.)

The Duke and Duchess of Windsor on their wedding day, June 3, 1937 (Popperfoto, Getty Images)

The Windsors with Adolf Hitler, Berchtesgaden, October 1937 (Popperfoto, Getty Images)

Count Ciano and Joachim von Ribbentrop, Munich, October 1938 (Hulton Archive, Getty Images)

George VI and Queen Elizabeth, guests of President and Mrs Roosevelt, with the President's mother, Hyde Park, June 1939 (Hulton Archive, Getty Images)

Sumner Welles and Joseph P. Kennedy, London, March 1940 (Hulton Archive, Getty Images)

The Duke of Windsor, Governor-General of the Bahamas, and the Duchess, at home, January 1941 (David E. Scherman, *Life* magazine, Getty Images)